Easy-to-Make
Bible Story Puppets

by Valerie Bendt

Puppet Designs by Michelle DeMicco

Text Copyright 2005, by Valerie Bendt

Illustrations Copyright 2005, by Michelle DeMicco

Cover Photos and Cover Design by Melissa Bendt

Proof Read by Mandy Bendt

ISBN: 1885814-17-8

Published by Bendt Family Ministries

333 W. Rio Vista Court

Tampa, FL 33604-6940

813-758-6793

www.ValerieBendt.com

Table of Contents:

Introduction

Children love to pretend. They can imitate people, animals, and events in the world around them. As your child pretends, you may recognize some of the phrases that she uses as your own. For instance, you may hear her talking to her doll or puppet saying, "It's time for your nap now. No crying. You can play outside when you wake up."

Imaginary play allows a child to have complete control over a situation. She dictates naptime, dinnertime, playtime, and so on. It allows her to try out different life experiences. She can be a mother at one moment and a tiger in the jungle at another. She can travel to far away places and times.

Children have extraordinary imaginations. Their creativity is enhanced through dramatic play, using puppets, dolls, and stuffed animals. A favorite pastime of my young children is to act out scenes from books we are reading together. I am pleased they can *pretend* at their books. They are not held hostage by the latest TV fad, only capable of imitating the mundane responses of the shallow characters they portray.

We as parents can encourage dramatic play by providing a variety of materials. These props do not need to be expensive or elaborate. My children have always enjoyed the games and toys that I have made for them as well as, or even better than, those I have purchased. I believe the reason for this is twofold. When I make a toy or game, I am investing time and energy in my children. This tells them that they are important to me. Also, in many instances, they are able to help make the items. This is both fun and educational. My children value the time we spend together. The second reason I believe children often like home-made props better than items purchased from a store is because they better stimulate their imaginations. Pretending depends on a certain amount of creativity. It is fun to invent ways to create a make-believe world.

The puppet patterns in this book are designed to be both entertaining, educational, and spiritually uplifting. Hand puppets are easy for children to use. They enjoy acting out scenes from their favorite Bible stories, thus aiding in memory retention, vocabulary development, and language skills. The puppets are inexpensive and easy to make, making them a truly valuable resource. I hope you will have as much fun making the puppets and reenacting stories from Bible with your children as I have had with mine.

Many of the puppets in this book can be used to represent a number of different Bible story characters. For example, the king puppet can be used to represent King Darius in the story of Daniel in the Lions Den, King Ahasuerus in the story of Esther, or King Herod in the story of the birth of the Messiah. I have provided a list of Bible story characters for each puppet. Feel free to use the puppets to retell any story from the Bible that interests you. Color photographs of each puppet appear on the outside and inside book covers. You may choose to use different colors of felt to create variety in clothing, hair color, and skin color. The puppets can serve as felt board characters as well. Another idea is to enable the children to play with the puppets as felt dolls. You can glue a felt body and face to a puppet background or even to a plain felt square. Draw facial features on the puppet face. Then cut out a variety of hair styles and clothing for the children to "stick" on the puppet body. These felt dolls can be used again and again.

The puppets in this book were designed by my oldest daughter, Michelle. Michelle was homeschooled all of her school life. She now has two children of her own. It is fun to take part in the home education of a second generation! Michelle also designed the puppets in our first puppet book, ***Successful Puppet Making***, which contains patterns and directions for creating 24 animal puppets. (See page 179 for details about this book.)

General Directions for Making the Puppets

The puppets can be made from colored felt squares or heavy weight colored construction paper. Felt produces durable puppets; however, construction paper is less expensive and easier to cut for mass production for a group project.

The fronts and backs of the felt puppets are sewed together using a large embroidery needle and a length of embroidery thread. The puppets' features such as body, head, clothes, and hair are cut from felt and are attached with fabric glue. I prefer to use Aleene's OK To Wash-It brand fabric glue, which provides a permanent fabric bond. Since the felt puppets must be sewn with a real needle and thread, you will need to assist children with this task, or you may want to do it yourself. I was pleasantly surprised to find that most of the children I have worked with have been able to sew the puppets with adult supervision – even children as young as four years old.

The fronts and backs of the construction paper puppets can be laced together by using a large plastic needle and a strand of embroidery thread. After the construction paper puppets are cut out, a series of holes can be made around the perimeter of the puppets by using a hole punch. A large plastic needle can be threaded with embroidery thread and then laced through the pre-punched holes in the puppets. (A cotton-tipped swab can be substituted for a plastic needle. Simply tie the thread to the swab and lace it through the pre-punched holes.) This activity can be done by young children. The puppets' features can be cut from construction paper and attached with glue sticks or Elmer's glue.

Whatever puppet variety you choose to make, your children can assist you with gluing the features onto the puppets. Best of all, they can play with the puppets when they are finished! Choose a puppet you want to make. Locate the puppet pattern in the back of the book, and either photocopy the pattern or trace it. You may choose to cut eyes, noses, and mouths out of felt, or you may choose to draw on these features with three-dimensional fabric paint or a permanent marker. Be sure to practice drawing the facial features on a scrap piece of felt before attempting to draw these features on your finished puppet. I have found it helpful to apply spray starch and a warm iron to the felt used to make the faces. This makes it much easier to paint or draw on the faces.

Follow the directions for making the puppet you have selected. Each puppet requires two felt squares for the background and a variety of colored felt scraps for the clothing and accessories. We have chosen to make all of our puppet backgrounds light blue. This helps them to blend in with a light blue sky background, thus allowing the actual characters to stand out.

All the materials required to make the puppets are available at either Wal-Mart, arts and crafts stores, or fabric stores. Be sure to purchase extra felt and embroidery thread to make allowances for "mistakes."

Puppets make great gifts! Children can make a puppet or two for a friend's birthday. Homemade gifts are a treasure, as well as an economical choice.

Directions for Sewing the Puppets

Each puppet is glued to a puppet background which is first hand sewn. All of the people puppets are glued to the puppet background as shown below. The pattern for this puppet background is found on page 133. Trace or photocopy the pattern, and cut it out. Place two colored felt squares together, one on top of the other. (We have chosen light blue felt for all of the puppet backgrounds.) Then place the puppet background pattern piece on top of the felt squares, pin, and cut around the pattern piece through both layers of felt.

Thread a large embroidery needle with a 5 foot strand of embroidery thread, and tie a knot in one end of the thread. (Do not separate the strands of embroidery thread.) Sew the edges of the puppet background together. Begin at the bottom edge as shown in the diagram. Work your way around the outer edge, always inserting your needle on the back side and pulling it out on the front side of the puppet background. Do not stitch across the bottom edge of the puppet background. When finished, secure the stitches by making two or three overlapping stitches. Cut away the excess thread.

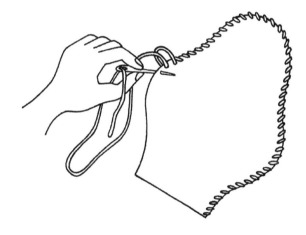

Some of the wider puppets, such as animal puppets, are glued to the puppet background shown below. The pattern for this puppet background is found on page 134.

Some of the puppets are rather large for a child's small hands. If you like you can place a felt piece inside the puppets to create a better fit for small hands. The small hand pattern piece as shown below is found on page 135.

Cut a single piece of felt from the pattern piece found on page 135. Place a line of fabric glue around the outside edge (not across the bottom edge) and glue the felt piece inside the finished puppet. The child's small hand will fit comfortably inside this insert.

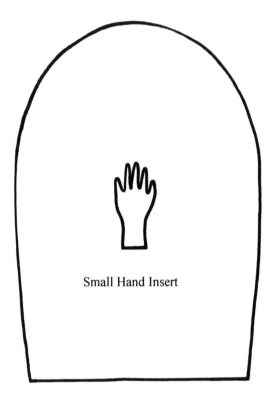

Small Hand Insert

Directions for Making Puppet Scenes

You may want to make puppet scenes to use as a backdrop when acting out Bible stories. Each scene on the next five pages can be enlarged at most any copy center to fit 11" X 17" paper. Children enjoy coloring the scenes. You can glue the finished scenes onto cardboard or have them laminated for durability. Fold the paper as shown below to enable the scenes to stand on a table. This size scene works well for you and your children to use at home when retelling Bible stories.

The scenes can also be enlarged to a greater size of about 15" X 24" at a copy center such as FedEx Kinko's. This may be desirable for putting on productions for a large group. These scenes can be glued onto cardboard or laminated for durability.

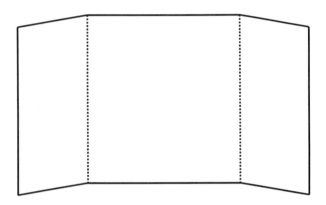

Key for puppet scenes:
A – Water for flood. Place this over the land in scene "B" to show ark floating on water.
B – Noah's ark before and after the flood.
C – Garden of Eden.
D – Jonah takes a ship to avoid going to Nineveh, or any boat scene.
E – Farm scene such as farm where the Prodigal Son feeds the pigs.
F – Calvary and the empty tomb.
G – Stable scene at the birth of the Messiah.
H – Pasture scene such as where David tends his sheep or where the Messiah preaches to the multitudes, or where the shepherd looks for his lost sheep.
I – Battle scene between David and Goliath including the brook where David gathers the five stones for his sling.
J – Lion's den in the story of Daniel.
K – River where Baby Moses is placed in his basket boat; any scene that requires a river.
L – Pit into which Joseph is thrown by his jealous brothers; could also be used as a well.
M – Palace of a king or queen.
N – Passover meal.
O – Granaries in Egypt.

A

B

C

D

E

F

13

G

H

I

J

K

L

15

M

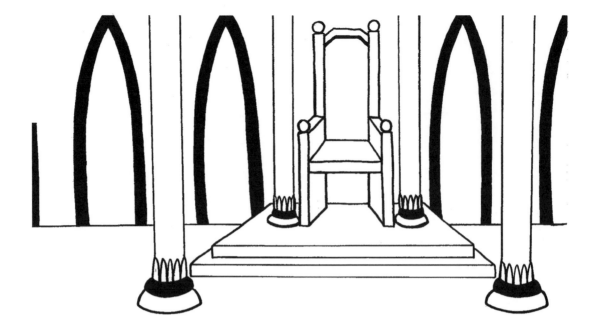

N

O

Baby Moses

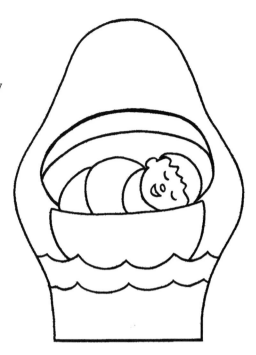

Possible Characters: Baby Moses. The baby can be used as any baby in a cradle if you omit the basket lid and the water.

Materials:

- 2 light blue felt squares for puppet background

- 1 tan felt square for basket boat

- Peach colored felt scraps for baby's face

- Brown colored felt scraps for baby's hair

- 1 medium blue colored felt square for baby blanket, baby body, and water

- Light blue embroidery thread

- Scissors

- Straight pins or masking tape

- Large tapestry needle, size 18 or 20

- Fabric glue

- Puppet Background A on page 133. Pattern pieces 7 B, 7 C, 7 D, 7 E on page 142. Pattern pieces 25 B on page 160; 26 B on page 161; 27 B, 27 C, and 27 D on page 162.

Directions:

Sew the puppet background according to the directions on page 9. Photocopy or trace the Baby Moses pattern pieces, and cut them out. Pin or tape the pattern pieces to the felt, and then cut out the felt. Rolled pieces of masking tape can be attached at several points to the back of each pattern piece. This will enable the pattern piece to stick to the felt while cutting. Follow the directions beside each diagram for cutting and gluing the pattern pieces. You may want to cut out all the felt pieces, and practice placing them on the puppet before gluing each piece in place.

Attach pattern pieces 27 B, 27 C, and 27 D to the tan felt, and cut out the felt. Remove pattern piece 27 B from the tan felt. Cover one side of the felt with fabric glue, and glue the felt piece on the puppet as shown in the diagram. Save pattern pieces 27 C and 27 D for later.

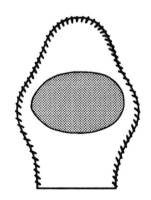

Remove pattern piece 27 D from the tan felt. Cover one side of the felt with fabric glue, and glue the felt piece on the puppet as shown in the diagram.

Attach pattern pieces 7 B and 7 E to the medium blue felt, and cut out the felt. Remove pattern piece 7 B from the medium blue felt. Cover one side of the felt with fabric glue, and glue the felt piece on the puppet as shown in the diagram. Save pattern piece 7 E for the next step.

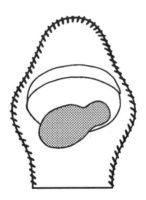

Remove pattern piece 7 E from the medium blue felt. Cover one side of the felt with fabric glue, and glue the felt piece on the puppet as shown in the diagram.

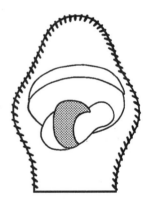

Attach pattern piece 7 C to the peach felt, and cut out the felt. Remove the pattern piece from the felt. Cover one side of the felt with fabric glue, and glue the felt piece on the puppet as shown in the diagram.

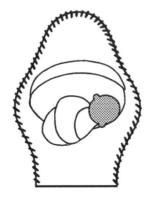

Easy-to-Make Bible Story Puppets

Attach pattern piece 7 D to the brown felt, and cut out the felt. Remove the pattern piece from the felt. Cover one side of the felt with fabric glue, and glue the felt piece on the puppet as shown in the diagram.

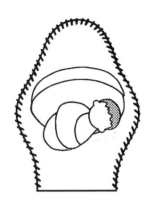

Remove pattern piece 27 C from the tan felt, and cut out the felt. Remove the pattern piece from the felt. Cover one side of the felt with fabric glue, and glue the felt piece on the puppet as shown in the diagram.

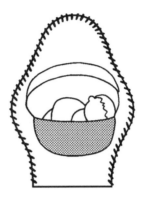

Attach pattern piece 26 B to the medium blue felt, and cut out the felt. Remove the pattern piece from the felt. Cover one side of the felt with fabric glue, and glue the felt piece on the puppet as shown in the diagram.

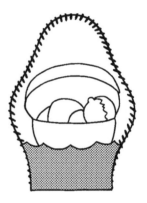

Attach pattern piece 25B to the medium blue felt, and cut out the felt. Remove the pattern piece from the felt. Cover one side of the felt with fabric glue, and glue the felt piece on the puppet as shown in the diagram.

Add facial features using three-dimensional fabric paint, permanent markers, or felt scraps.

Baby Jesus (Yeshua)

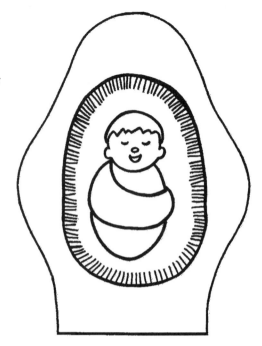

Possible Characters: Baby Jesus. The baby can be used as any baby if you omit the bed of hay. The baby can be made without a puppet background and can be held by another puppet.

Materials:

- 2 light blue felt squares for puppet background
- 1 yellow felt square for bed of hay
- Peach colored felt scraps for baby's face
- Brown colored felt scraps for baby's hair
- 1 medium blue colored felt square for baby blanket and baby's body
- Light blue embroidery thread
- Scissors
- Straight pins or masking tape
- Large tapestry needle, size 18 or 20
- Fabric glue
- Puppet Background A on page 133. Pattern pieces 7 A, 7 B, 7 C, 7 D, and 7 E on page 142.

Directions:

Sew the puppet background according to the directions on page 9. Photocopy or trace the Baby Jesus pieces, and cut them out. Pin or tape the pattern pieces to the felt, and then cut out the felt. Rolled pieces of masking tape can be attached at several points to the back of each pattern piece. This will enable the pattern piece to stick to the felt while cutting. Follow the directions beside each diagram for cutting and gluing the pattern pieces. You may want to cut out all the felt pieces, and practice placing them on the puppet before gluing each piece in place.

Attach pattern piece 7A to the yellow felt, and cut out the felt. Remove the pattern piece from the felt. Cut a ring of fringe around the felt piece as indicated in the diagram and as shown on the pattern piece. Cover one side of the felt with fabric glue, leaving the fringed parts free from glue. Glue the felt piece on the puppet as shown in the diagram.

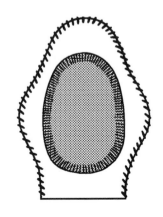

Easy-to-Make Bible Story Puppets

Attach pattern pieces 7 B and 7 E to the medium blue felt, and cut out the felt. Remove pattern piece 7 B from the medium blue felt. Cover one side of the felt with fabric glue, and glue the felt piece on the puppet as shown in the diagram. Save pattern piece 7 E for the next step.

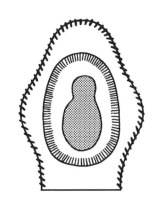

Remove pattern piece 7 E from the medium blue felt. Cover one side of the felt with fabric glue, and glue the felt piece on the puppet as shown in the diagram.

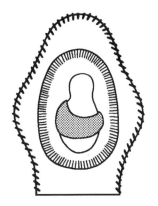

Attach pattern piece 7 C to the peach felt, and cut out the felt. Remove the pattern piece from the felt. Cover one side of the felt with fabric glue, and glue the felt piece on the puppet as shown in the diagram.

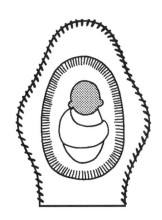

Attach pattern piece 7 D to the brown felt, and cut out the felt. Remove the pattern piece from the felt. Cover one side of the felt with fabric glue, and glue the felt piece on the puppet as shown in the diagram.

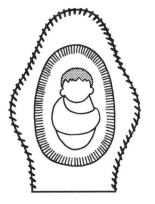

Add facial features using three-dimensional fabric paint, permanent markers, or felt scraps.

Angel

Possible Characters: Angel at the birth of the Messiah or the Angel in the Fiery Furnace. Can be the Angel Gabriel if you use the wings with a male puppet wearing robe 16 B. Make robe 16 B 1/2" longer to cover puppet's feet.

Materials:

- 2 light blue felt squares for puppet background
- Peach colored felt square for body and face
- Yellow felt scraps for hair
- White felt square for wings and collar
- Yellow felt square for dress
- Light blue embroidery thread
- Scissors
- Straight pins or masking tape
- Large tapestry needle, size 18 or 20
- Fabric glue
- Puppet Background A on page 133. Pattern pieces 2 A, 2 C, and 2 G on page 137. Pattern pieces 8 A, 8 B, and 8 C on page 143.

Directions:

Sew the puppet background according to the directions on page 9. Photocopy or trace the Angel pattern pieces, and cut them out. Pin or tape the pattern pieces to the felt, and then cut out the felt. Rolled pieces of masking tape can be attached at several points to the back of each pattern piece. This will enable the pattern piece to stick to the felt while cutting. Follow the directions beside each diagram for cutting and gluing the pattern pieces. You may want to cut out all the felt pieces, and practice placing them on the puppet before gluing each piece in place.

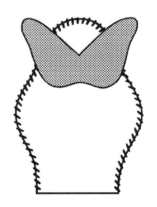

Attach pattern piece 8 A to the white felt, and cut out the felt. Remove the pattern from the felt. Cover one side of the felt with fabric glue, and glue the felt piece on the puppet as shown in the diagram. A portion of the wing piece will overhang the puppet background, so do not apply glue to this part.

Attach pattern pieces 2 A and 2 C to the peach felt, and cut out the felt. Remove pattern piece 2 A from the peach felt. Cover one side of the felt with fabric glue, and glue the felt piece on the puppet as shown in the diagram. Save pattern piece 2 C for the next step.

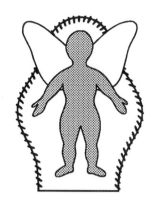

Remove pattern piece 2 C from the peach felt. Cover one side of the felt with fabric glue, and glue the felt piece on the puppet as shown in the diagram.

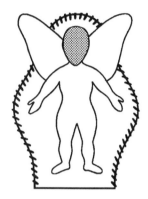

Attach pattern piece 8 C to the yellow felt, and cut out the felt. Remove the pattern piece from the felt. Cover one side of the felt with fabric glue, and glue the felt piece on the puppet as shown in the diagram.

Attach pattern piece 8 B to the white felt, and cut out the felt. Remove the pattern piece from the felt. Cover one side of the felt with fabric glue, and glue the felt piece on the puppet as shown in the diagram.

Attach pattern piece 2 G to the yellow felt, and cut out the felt. Remove the pattern piece from the felt. Cover one side of the felt with fabric glue, and glue the felt piece on the puppet as shown in the diagram.

Add facial features using three-dimensional fabric paint, permanent markers, or felt scraps.

Easy-to-Make Bible Story Puppets

Maid

Possible Characters: Esther before she becomes queen or any young woman.

Materials:

- 2 light blue felt squares for puppet background
- Peach colored felt square for body and face
- Pink felt square for dress
- White felt scraps for headband and belt
- Yellow felt scraps for hair
- Black felt scraps for shoes
- Light blue embroidery thread
- Scissors
- Straight pins or masking tape
- Large tapestry needle, size 18 or 20
- Fabric glue
- Puppet Background A on page 133. Pattern pieces 2 A, 2 B, 2 C, 2 D, 2 F, 2 H, and 2 I on page 137. Pattern piece 9 B on page 144.

Directions:

Sew the puppet background according to the directions on page 9. Photocopy or trace the Maid pattern pieces, and cut them out. Pin or tape the pattern pieces to the felt, and then cut out the felt. Rolled pieces of masking tape can be attached at several points to the back of each pattern piece. This will enable the pattern piece to stick to the felt while cutting. Follow the directions beside each diagram for cutting and gluing the pattern pieces. You may want to cut out all the felt pieces, and practice placing them on the puppet before gluing each piece in place.

Attach pattern pieces 2 A and 2 C to the peach felt, and cut out the felt. Remove pattern piece 2 A from the peach felt. Cover one side of the felt with fabric glue, and glue the felt piece on the puppet as shown in the diagram. Save pattern piece 2 C for the next step.

Remove pattern piece 2 C from the peach felt. Cover one side of the felt with fabric glue, and glue the felt piece on the puppet as shown in the diagram.

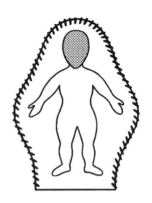

Attach pattern pieces 2 H and 2 I to the black felt, and cut out the felt. Remove the pattern pieces from the felt. Cover one side of the felt with fabric glue, and glue the felt pieces on the puppet as shown in the diagram.

Attach pattern piece 9 B to the pink felt, and cut out the felt. Remove the pattern piece from the felt. Cover one side of the felt with fabric glue, and glue the felt piece on the puppet as shown in the diagram.

Attach pattern piece 2 B to the yellow felt, and cut out the felt. Remove the pattern piece from the felt. Cover one side of the felt with fabric glue, and glue the felt piece on the puppet as shown in the diagram.

Easy-to-Make Bible Story Puppets

Attach pattern piece 2 D and 2 F to the white felt, and cut out the felt. Remove the pattern pieces from the felt. Cover one side of the felt with fabric glue, and glue the felt pieces on the puppet as shown in the diagram.

Add facial features using three-dimensional fabric paint, permanent markers, or felt scraps.

Egyptian Princess

Possible Characters: Egyptian Princess or Egyptian Queen.

Materials:

- 2 light blue felt squares for puppet background
- Tan colored felt square for body and face
- Black felt scraps for hair and shoes
- Yellow felt square for dress, trimming, and headdress
- Medium blue felt square for headdress, dress trimming, and belt
- Light blue embroidery thread
- Scissors
- Straight pins or masking tape
- Large tapestry needle, size 18 or 20
- Fabric glue
- Puppet Background A on page 133. Pattern pieces 2 A, 2 B, 2 C, 2 H, and 2 I on page 137. Pattern pieces 12 A through 12 K on page 147.

Directions:

Sew the puppet background according to the directions on page 9. Photocopy or trace the Egyptian Princess pattern pieces, and cut them out. Pin or tape the pattern pieces to the felt, and then cut out the felt. Rolled pieces of masking tape can be attached at several points to the back of each pattern piece. This will enable the pattern piece to stick to the felt while cutting. Follow the directions beside each diagram for cutting and gluing the pattern pieces. You may want to cut out all the felt pieces, and practice placing them on the puppet before gluing each piece in place.

Attach pattern pieces 2 A and 2 C to the tan felt, and cut out the felt. Remove pattern piece 2 A from the tan felt. Cover one side of the felt with fabric glue, and glue the felt piece on the puppet as shown in the diagram. Save pattern piece 2 C for later.

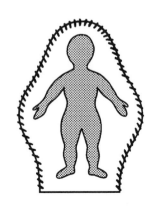

Attach pattern pieces 2 H and 2 I to the black felt, and cut out the felt. Remove the pattern pieces from the felt. Cover one side of the felt with fabric glue, and glue the felt pieces on the puppet as shown in the diagram.

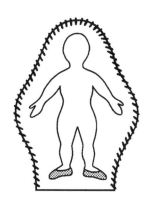

Attach pattern piece 12 J to the yellow felt, and cut out the felt. Remove the pattern piece from the felt. Cover one side of the felt with fabric glue, and glue the felt piece on the puppet as shown in the diagram.

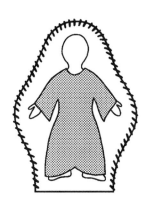

Attach pattern pieces 12 H, 12 I, and 12 K to the medium blue felt, and cut out the felt. Remove the pattern pieces from the felt. Cover one side of the felt with fabric glue, and glue the felt pieces on the puppet as shown in the diagram.

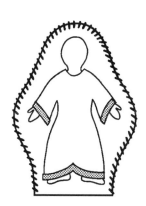

Attach pattern piece 12 F to the yellow felt, and cut out the felt. Remove the pattern piece from the felt. Cover one side of the felt with fabric glue, and glue the felt piece on the puppet as shown in the diagram.

Attach pattern piece 12 G and pattern piece 12 E to the medium blue felt, and cut out the felt. Remove the pattern pieces from the felt. Cover one side of the felt with fabric glue, and glue the felt pieces on the puppet as shown in the diagram.

Attach pattern piece 12 B to the yellow felt, and cut out the felt. Remove the pattern piece from the felt. Cover one side of the felt with fabric glue, and glue the felt piece on the puppet as shown in the diagram.

Attach pattern piece 2 B to the black felt, and cut out the felt. Remove the pattern piece from the felt. Cover one side of the felt with fabric glue, and glue the felt piece on the puppet as shown in the diagram.

Attach pattern piece 12 D to the medium blue felt, and cut out the felt. Remove the pattern piece from the felt. Cover one side of the felt with fabric glue, and glue the felt piece on the puppet as shown in the diagram.

Easy-to-Make Bible Story Puppets

Remove pattern piece 2 C from the tan felt. Cover one side of the felt with fabric glue, and glue the felt piece on the puppet as shown in the diagram.

Attach pattern piece 12 A to the medium blue felt, and cut out the felt. Remove the pattern piece from the felt. Cover one side of the felt with fabric glue, and glue the felt piece on the puppet as shown in the diagram.

Attach pattern piece 12 C to the yellow felt, and cut out the felt. Remove the pattern piece from the felt. Cover one side of the felt with fabric glue, and glue the felt piece on the puppet as shown in the diagram. Add facial features and stripes on headdress and sash using three-dimensional fabric paint, permanent markers, yarn, or felt scraps.

Eve

Materials:

- 2 light blue felt squares for puppet background
- Peach colored felt square for body and face
- Green felt square for leaf garment
- Brown felt square for animal skin garment (optional)
- Brown felt scraps for hair
- Light blue embroidery thread
- Scissors
- Straight pins or masking tape
- Large tapestry needle, size 18 or 20
- Fabric glue
- Puppet Background A on page 133. Pattern pieces 2 A, 2 B, and 2 C on page 137. Pattern piece 10 A on page 145.

Directions:

Sew the puppet background according to the directions on page 9. Photocopy or trace the Eve pattern pieces, and cut them out. Pin or tape the pattern pieces to the felt, and then cut out the felt. Rolled pieces of masking tape can be attached at several points to the back of each pattern piece. This will enable the pattern piece to stick to the felt while cutting. Follow the directions beside each diagram for cutting and gluing the pattern pieces. You may want to cut out all the felt pieces, and practice placing them on the puppet before gluing each piece in place.

Attach pattern pieces 2 A and 2 C to the peach felt, and cut out the felt. Remove pattern piece 2 A from the peach felt. Cover one side of the felt with fabric glue, and glue the felt piece on the puppet as shown in the diagram. Save pattern piece 2 C for the next step.

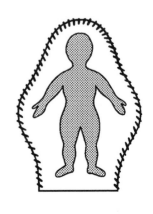

Remove pattern piece 2 C from the peach felt. Cover one side of the felt with fabric glue, and glue the felt piece on the puppet as shown in the diagram.

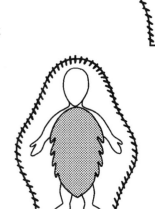

Attach pattern piece 10 A to the green felt, and cut out the felt. Remove the pattern piece from the felt. Cover one side of the felt with fabric glue, and glue the felt piece on the puppet as shown in the diagram. (You may choose to make an animal skin garment using the same pattern cut from brown felt. This can be placed over the leaf garment to indicate when the Lord made clothes for Adam and Eve out of animal skins. This does not need to be glued on but can simply be added by attaching a piece of rolled masking tape to the back of the brown felt piece.)

Add lines for leaf veins using three-dimensional fabric paint, permanent markers, yarn, or felt scraps.

Attach pattern piece 2 B to the brown felt, and cut out the felt. Remove the pattern piece from the felt. Cover one side of the felt with fabric glue, and glue the felt piece on the puppet as shown in the diagram.

Add facial features using three-dimensional fabric paint, permanent markers, or felt scraps.

Miriam

Possible Characters: Miriam or any peasant girl.

Materials:

- 2 light blue felt squares for puppet background
- Peach colored felt square for body and face
- Green felt square for dress
- Yellow felt scraps for headband and sash
- Brown felt scraps for hair
- Black felt scraps for shoes
- Light blue embroidery thread
- Scissors
- Straight pins or masking tape
- Large tapestry needle, size 18 or 20
- Fabric glue
- Puppet Background A on page 133. Pattern pieces 4 A, 4 B, 4 C, 4 D, 4 E, 4 F, 4 G, and 4 H on page 139.

Directions:

Sew the puppet background according to the directions on page 9. Photocopy or trace the Miriam pattern pieces, and cut them out. Pin or tape the pattern pieces to the felt, and then cut out the felt. Rolled pieces of masking tape can be attached at several points to the back of each pattern piece. This will enable the pattern piece to stick to the felt while cutting. Follow the directions beside each diagram for cutting and gluing the pattern pieces. You may want to cut out all the felt pieces, and practice placing them on the puppet before gluing each piece in place.

Attach pattern pieces 4 A and 4 B to the peach felt, and cut out the felt. Remove pattern piece 4 A from the peach felt. Cover one side of the felt with fabric glue, and glue the felt piece on the puppet as shown in the diagram. Save pattern piece 4 B for later.

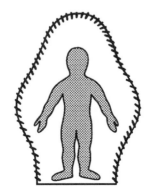

Easy-to-Make Bible Story Puppets

Remove pattern piece 4 B from the peach felt. Cover one side of the felt with fabric glue, and glue the felt piece on the puppet as shown in the diagram.

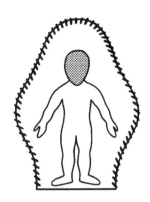

Attach pattern piece 4 D to the green felt, and cut out the felt. Remove the pattern piece from the felt. Cover one side of the felt with fabric glue, and glue the felt piece on the puppet as shown in the diagram.

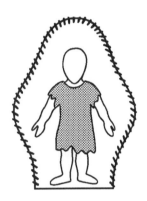

Attach pattern piece 4 C to the yellow felt, and cut out the felt. Remove the pattern piece from the felt. Cover one side of the felt with fabric glue, and glue the felt piece on the puppet as shown in the diagram.

Attach pattern piece 4 E to the brown felt, and cut out the felt. Remove the pattern piece from the felt. Cover one side of the felt with fabric glue, and glue the felt piece on the puppet as shown in the diagram.

Attach pattern pieces 4 G and 4 H to the black felt, and cut out the felt. Remove the pattern pieces from the felt. Cover one side of the felt with fabric glue, and glue the felt pieces on the puppet as shown in the diagram.

Attach pattern piece 4 F to the yellow felt, and cut out the felt. Remove the pattern piece from the felt. Cover one side of the felt with fabric glue, and glue the felt piece on the puppet as shown in the diagram. Add facial features using three-dimensional fabric paint, permanent markers, or felt scraps.

Girl

Possible Characters: Any young girl in either the Old or New Testament, the young girl healed by the Messiah who was thought by her family to be dead, or one of the girls in the story where the Lord admonishes his disciples to "Let the children come unto me and forbid them not."

Materials:

- 2 light blue felt squares for puppet background
- Peach colored felt square for body and face
- Lavender felt square for dress
- Pink felt scraps for headband and sash
- Yellow felt scraps for hair
- Black felt scraps for shoes
- Light blue embroidery thread
- Scissors
- Straight pins or masking tape
- Large tapestry needle, size 18 or 20
- Fabric glue
- Puppet Background A on page 133. Pattern pieces 4 A, 4 B, 4 G, and 4 H on page 139. Pattern pieces 5 A, 5 B, 5 C, 5 D, 5 E, and 5 F on page 140.

Directions:

Sew the puppet background according to the directions on page 9. Photocopy or trace the Girl pattern pieces, and cut them out. Pin or tape the pattern pieces to the felt, and then cut out the felt. Rolled pieces of masking tape can be attached at several points to the back of each pattern piece. This will enable the pattern piece to stick to the felt while cutting. Follow the directions beside each diagram for cutting and gluing the pattern pieces. You may want to cut out all the felt pieces, and practice placing them on the puppet before gluing each piece in place.

Attach pattern pieces 4 A and 4 B to the peach felt, and cut out the felt. Remove pattern piece 4 A from the peach felt. Cover one side of the felt with fabric glue, and glue the felt piece on the puppet as shown in the diagram. Save pattern piece 4 B for later.

Attach pattern piece 5 A to the lavender felt, and cut out the felt. Remove the pattern piece from the felt. Cover one side of the felt with fabric glue, and glue the felt piece on the puppet as shown in the diagram.

Remove pattern piece 4 B from the peach felt. Cover one side of the felt with fabric glue, and glue the felt piece on the puppet as shown in the diagram.

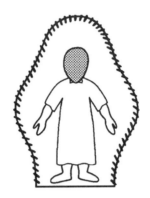

Attach pattern piece 5 B to the yellow felt, and cut out the felt. Remove the pattern piece from the felt. Cover one side of the felt with fabric glue, and glue the felt piece on the puppet as shown in the diagram.

Attach pattern pieces 4 G and 4 H to the black felt, and cut out the felt. Remove the pattern pieces from the felt. Cover one side of the felt with fabric glue, and glue the felt pieces on the puppet as shown in the diagram.

Easy-to-Make Bible Story Puppets

Attach pattern pieces 5 C and 5 D to the pink felt, and cut out the felt. Remove the pattern pieces from the felt. Cover one side of the felt with fabric glue, and glue the felt piece on the puppet as shown in the diagram.

Attach pattern pieces 5 E and 5 F to the pink felt, and cut out the felt. Remove the pattern pieces from the felt. Cover one side of the felt with fabric glue, and glue the felt pieces on the puppet as shown in the diagram.

Add facial features using three-dimensional fabric paint, permanent markers, or felt scraps.

Mary (Mother of Jesus)

Possible Characters: Mary or any woman who is "with child."

Materials:

- 2 light blue felt squares for puppet background
- Peach colored felt square for body and face
- Medium blue felt square for dress and headdress
- White felt scraps for belt
- Brown felt scraps for hair
- Black felt scraps for shoes
- Light blue embroidery thread
- Scissors
- Straight pins or masking tape
- Large tapestry needle, size 18 or 20
- Fabric glue
- Puppet Background A on page 133. Pattern pieces 2 A, 2 C, 2 E, 2 G, 2 H, and 2 I on page 137. Pattern pieces 11A, and 11 B on page 146.

Directions:

Sew the puppet background according to the directions on page 9. Photocopy or trace the Mary pattern pieces, and cut them out. Pin or tape the pattern pieces to the felt, and then cut out the felt. Rolled pieces of masking tape can be attached at several points to the back of each pattern piece. This will enable the pattern piece to stick to the felt while cutting. Follow the directions beside each diagram for cutting and gluing the pattern pieces. You may want to cut out all the felt pieces, and practice placing them on the puppet before gluing each piece in place.

Attach pattern pieces 2 A and 2 C to the peach felt, and cut out the felt. Remove pattern piece 2 A from the peach felt. Cover one side of the felt with fabric glue, and glue the felt piece on the puppet as shown in the diagram. Save pattern piece 2 C for the next step.

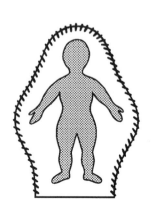

Easy-to-Make Bible Story Puppets

Remove pattern piece 2 C from the peach felt. Cover one side of the felt with fabric glue, and glue the felt piece on the puppet as shown in the diagram.

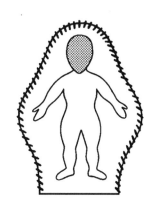

Attach pattern pieces 2 H and 2 I to the black felt, and cut out the felt. Remove the pattern pieces from the felt. Cover one side of the felt with fabric glue, and glue the felt pieces on the puppet as shown in the diagram.

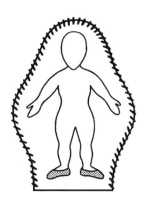

Attach pattern piece 11 A to the medium blue felt, and cut out the felt. Remove the pattern piece from the felt. Cover one side of the felt with fabric glue, and glue the felt piece on the puppet as shown in the diagram.

Attach pattern piece 2 E to the white felt, and cut out the felt. Remove the pattern piece from the felt. Cover one side of the felt with fabric glue, and glue the felt piece on the puppet as shown in the diagram.

Attach pattern piece 2 G to the brown felt, and cut out the felt. Remove the pattern piece from the felt. Cover one side of the felt with fabric glue, and glue the felt piece on the puppet as shown in the diagram.

Attach pattern piece 11 B to the medium blue felt, and cut out the felt. Remove the pattern piece from the felt. Cover one side of the felt with fabric glue, and glue the felt piece on the puppet as shown in the diagram.

Add facial features using three-dimensional fabric paint, permanent markers, or felt scraps.

Easy-to-Make Bible Story Puppets

Jochebed (Mother of Moses)

Possible Characters: Jochebed, the sisters Mary and Martha in the New Testament, or any woman in the Old or New Testament.

Materials:

- 2 light blue felt squares for puppet background

- Peach colored felt square for body and face

- Green felt square for dress

- Tan felt scraps for headdress and sash

- Gray felt scraps for hair (brown or yellow hair for a younger woman)

- Black felt scraps for shoes

- Light blue embroidery thread

- Scissors

- Straight pins or masking tape

- Large tapestry needle, size 18 or 20

- Fabric glue

- Puppet Background A on page 133. Pattern pieces 2 A, 2 B, 2 C, 2 H, and 2 I on page 137. Pattern pieces 10 B, and 10 C on page 145. Pattern piece 11 B on page 146.

Directions:

Sew the puppet background according to the directions on page 9. Photocopy or trace the Jochebed pattern pieces, and cut them out. Pin or tape the pattern pieces to the felt, and then cut out the felt. Rolled pieces of masking tape can be attached at several points to the back of each pattern piece. This will enable the pattern piece to stick to the felt while cutting. Follow the directions beside each diagram for cutting and gluing the pattern pieces. You may want to cut out all the felt pieces, and practice placing them on the puppet before gluing each piece in place.

Attach pattern pieces 2 A and 2 C to the peach felt, and cut out the felt. Remove pattern piece 2 A from the peach felt. Cover one side of the felt with fabric glue, and glue the felt piece on the puppet as shown in the diagram. Save pattern piece 2 C for the next step.

Remove pattern piece 2 C from the peach felt. Cover one side of the felt with fabric glue, and glue the felt piece on the puppet as shown in the diagram.

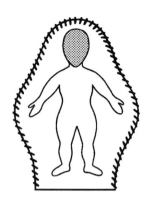

Attach pattern piece 10 B to the green felt, and cut out the felt. Remove the pattern piece from the felt. Cover one side of the felt with fabric glue, and glue the felt piece on the puppet as shown in the diagram.

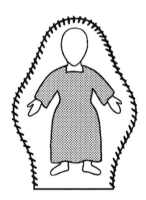

Attach pattern piece 10 C to the tan felt, and cut out the felt. Remove the pattern piece from the felt. Cover one side of the felt with fabric glue, and glue the felt piece on the puppet as shown in the diagram.

Attach pattern piece 2 B to the gray felt, and cut out the felt. Remove the pattern piece from the felt. Cover one side of the felt with fabric glue, and glue the felt piece on the puppet as shown in the diagram.

Easy-to-Make Bible Story Puppets

Attach pattern pieces 2 H and 2 I to the black felt, and cut out the felt. Remove the pattern pieces from the felt. Cover one side of the felt with fabric glue, and glue the felt pieces on the puppet as shown in the diagram.

Attach pattern piece 11 B to the tan felt, and cut out the felt. Remove the pattern piece from the felt. Cover one side of the felt with fabric glue, and glue the felt piece on the puppet as shown in the diagram. Add facial features using three-dimensional fabric paint, permanent markers, or felt scraps.

Queen Esther

Possible Characters: Queen Esther or any queen in the Old or New Testament. (See page 28 for the Egyptian Princess/Queen puppet.)

Materials:

- 2 light blue felt squares for puppet background
- Peach colored felt square for body and face
- Purple felt square for dress
- Yellow felt scraps for crown, collar, and belt
- Red felt scraps for jewels on crown and collar
- Brown felt scraps for hair
- Black felt scraps for shoes
- Light blue embroidery thread
- Scissors
- Straight pins or masking tape
- Large tapestry needle, size 18 or 20
- Fabric glue
- Puppet Background A on page 133. Pattern pieces 2 A, 2 B, 2 G, 2 H, and 2 I on page 137. Pattern pieces 9 A on page 144. Pattern pieces 11 C, 11 D, 11 E, 11 F, and 11 G on page 146.

Directions:

Sew the puppet background according to the directions on page 9. Photocopy or trace the Queen Esther pattern pieces, and cut them out. Pin or tape the pattern pieces to the felt, and then cut out the felt. Rolled pieces of masking tape can be attached at several points to the back of each pattern piece. This will enable the pattern piece to stick to the felt while cutting. Follow the directions beside each diagram for cutting and gluing the pattern pieces. You may want to cut out all the felt pieces, and practice placing them on the puppet before gluing each piece in place.

Attach pattern pieces 2 A and 2 C to the peach felt, and cut out the felt. Remove pattern piece 2 A from the peach felt. Cover one side of the felt with fabric glue, and glue the felt piece on the puppet as shown in the diagram. Save pattern piece 2 C for the next step.

Remove pattern piece 2 C from the peach felt. Cover one side of the felt with fabric glue, and glue the felt piece on the puppet as shown in the diagram.

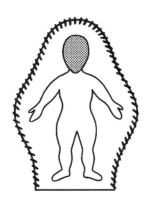

Attach pattern pieces 2 H and 2 I to the black felt, and cut out the felt. Remove the pattern pieces from the felt. Cover one side of the felt with fabric glue, and glue the felt pieces on the puppet as shown in the diagram.

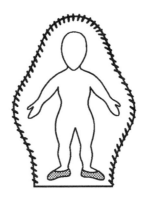

Attach pattern piece 9 A to the purple felt, and cut out the felt. Remove the pattern piece from the felt. Cover one side of the felt with fabric glue, and glue the felt piece on the puppet as shown in the diagram.

Attach pattern pieces 11 C and 11 E to the yellow felt, and cut out the felt. Remove the pattern pieces from the felt. Cover one side of the felt with fabric glue, and glue the felt pieces on the puppet as shown in the diagram.

Attach pattern pieces labeled 11 F to the red felt, and cut out the felt. Remove the pattern pieces from the felt. Cover one side of the felt with fabric glue, and glue the felt pieces on the puppet as shown in the diagram.

Attach pattern piece 2 G to the brown felt, and cut out the felt. Remove the pattern piece from the felt. Cover one side of the felt with fabric glue, and glue the felt piece on the puppet as shown in the diagram.

Attach pattern piece 11 D to the yellow felt, and cut out the felt. Remove the pattern piece from the felt. Cover one side of the felt with fabric glue, and glue the felt piece on the puppet as shown in the diagram.

Attach pattern pieces labeled 11 G to the red felt, and cut out the felt. Remove the pattern pieces from the felt. Cover one side of the felt with fabric glue, and glue the felt pieces on the crown as shown in the diagram. Add facial features using three-dimensional fabric paint, permanent markers, or felt scraps.

Joseph (Father of Jesus)

Possible Characters: Joseph the father of Jesus, a disciple of Christ, one of Joseph's brothers in the story of Joseph and his Coat of Many Colors, or any man in the Old or New Testament. Use a variety of felt colors and beard and head covering patterns to create multiple characters.

Materials:

- 2 light blue felt squares for puppet background

- Peach colored felt square for body and face

- Tan felt square for tunic and headband

- Green felt square for robe

- Brown felt scraps for hair and beard

- Black felt scraps for shoes

- Light blue embroidery thread

- Scissors

- Straight pins or masking tape

- Large tapestry needle, size 18 or 20

- Fabric glue

- Puppet Background A on page 133. Pattern pieces 1 A, 1 C, 1 D, and 1 E on page 136. Pattern pieces 6 C and 6 E on page 141. Pattern pieces 15 A and 15 B on page 150. Pattern piece 16 B on page 151.

Directions:

Sew the puppet background according to the directions on page 9. Photocopy or trace the Joseph pattern pieces, and cut them out. Pin or tape the pattern pieces to the felt, and then cut out the felt. Rolled pieces of masking tape can be attached at several points to the back of each pattern piece. This will enable the pattern piece to stick to the felt while cutting. Follow the directions beside each diagram for cutting and gluing the pattern pieces. You may want to cut out all the felt pieces, and practice placing them on the puppet before gluing each piece in place.

Attach pattern pieces 1 A and 1 C to the peach felt, and cut out the felt. Remove pattern piece 2 A from the peach felt. Cover one side of the felt with fabric glue, and glue the felt piece on the puppet as shown in the diagram. Save pattern piece 1 C for the next step.

Remove pattern piece 1 C from the peach felt. Cover one side of the felt with fabric glue, and glue the felt piece on the puppet as shown in the diagram.

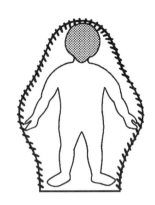

Attach pattern pieces 1 D and 1 E to the black felt, and cut out the felt. Remove the pattern pieces from the felt. Cover one side of the felt with fabric glue, and glue the felt pieces on the puppet as shown in the diagram.

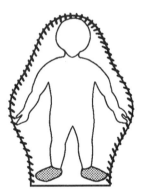

Attach pattern piece 16 B to the tan felt, and cut out the felt. Remove the pattern piece from the felt. Cover one side of the felt with fabric glue, and glue the felt piece on the puppet as shown in the diagram.

Attach pattern pieces 15 A and 15 B to the green felt, and cut out the felt. Remove the pattern pieces from the felt. Cover one side of the felt with fabric glue, and glue the felt pieces on the puppet as shown in the diagram.

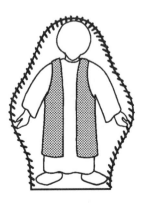

Easy-to-Make Bible Story Puppets

Attach pattern piece 6 C to the brown felt, and cut out the felt. Remove the pattern piece from the felt. Cover one side of the felt with fabric glue, and glue the felt piece on the puppet as shown in the diagram.

Attach pattern piece 6 E to the tan felt, and cut out the felt. Remove the pattern piece from the felt. Cover one side of the felt with fabric glue, and glue the felt piece on the puppet as shown in the diagram.

Add facial features using three-dimensional fabric paint, permanent markers, or felt scraps.

Noah

Possible Characters: Noah, Abraham, Simeon, Elijah, Wise Man, or any old man in the Old or New Testament.

Materials:

- 2 light blue felt squares for puppet background
- Peach colored felt square for body and face
- Tan felt square for tunic
- Brown felt square for robe
- Gray felt scraps for hair and beard
- Black felt scraps for shoes
- Light blue embroidery thread
- Scissors
- Straight pins or masking tape
- Large tapestry needle, size 18 or 20
- Fabric glue
- Puppet Background A on page 133. Pattern pieces 1 A, 1 C, 1 D, and 1 E on page 136. Pattern piece 6 A on page 141. Pattern pieces 16 A and 16 B on page 151.

Directions:

Sew the puppet background according to the directions on page 9. Photocopy or trace the Noah pattern pieces, and cut them out. Pin or tape the pattern pieces to the felt, and then cut out the felt. Rolled pieces of masking tape can be attached at several points to the back of each pattern piece. This will enable the pattern piece to stick to the felt while cutting. Follow the directions beside each diagram for cutting and gluing the pattern pieces. You may want to cut out all the felt pieces, and practice placing them on the puppet before gluing each piece in place.

Attach pattern pieces 1 A and 1 C to the peach felt, and cut out the felt. Remove pattern piece 1 A from the peach felt. Cover one side of the felt with fabric glue, and glue the felt piece on the puppet as shown in the diagram. Save pattern piece 1 C for the next step.

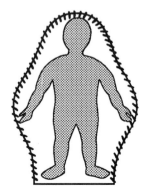

Easy-to-Make Bible Story Puppets

Remove pattern piece 1 C from the peach felt. Cover one side of the felt with fabric glue, and glue the felt piece on the puppet as shown in the diagram.

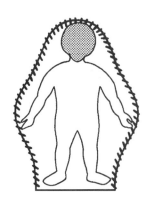

Attach pattern pieces 1 D and 1 E to the black felt, and cut out the felt. Remove the pattern pieces from the felt. Cover one side of the felt with fabric glue, and glue the felt pieces on the puppet as shown in the diagram.

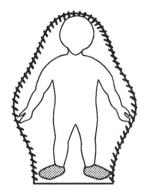

Attach pattern piece 16 B to the tan felt, and cut out the felt. Remove the pattern piece from the felt. Cover one side of the felt with fabric glue, and glue the felt piece on the puppet as shown in the diagram.

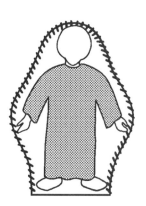

Attach pattern piece 16 A to the brown felt, and cut out the felt. Remove the pattern piece from the felt. Cover one side of the felt with fabric glue, and glue the felt piece on the puppet as shown in the diagram.

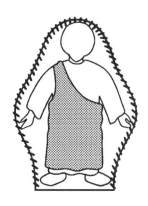

Attach pattern piece 6 A to the gray felt, and cut out the felt. Remove the pattern piece from the felt. Cover one side of the felt with fabric glue, and glue the felt piece on the puppet as shown in the diagram.

Add facial features using three-dimensional fabric paint, permanent markers, or felt scraps.

Easy-to-Make Bible Story Puppets

Moses with Tablets

Materials:

- 2 light blue felt squares for puppet background

- Peach colored felt square for body and face

- Orange felt square for tunic

- Tan felt square for robe

- White felt scraps for hair and beard

- Gray felt scraps for the stone tablets

- Black felt scraps for shoes

- Light blue embroidery thread

- Scissors

- Straight pins or masking tape

- Large tapestry needle, size 18 or 20

- Fabric glue

- Puppet Background A on page 133. Pattern pieces 1 A, 1 C, 1 D, and 1 E on page 136. Pattern piece 6 A on page 141. Pattern pieces 16 A and 16 B on page 151. Pattern piece 20 A on page 155.

Directions:

Sew the puppet background according to the directions on page 9. Photocopy or trace the Moses with Tablets pattern pieces, and cut them out. Pin or tape the pattern pieces to the felt, and then cut out the felt. Rolled pieces of masking tape can be attached at several points to the back of each pattern piece. This will enable the pattern piece to stick to the felt while cutting. Follow the directions beside each diagram for cutting and gluing the pattern pieces. You may want to cut out all the felt pieces, and practice placing them on the puppet before gluing each piece in place.

Attach pattern pieces 1 A and 1 C to the peach felt, and cut out the felt. Remove pattern piece 1 A from the peach felt. Cover one side of the felt with fabric glue, and glue the felt piece on the puppet as shown in the diagram. Save pattern piece 1 C for the next step.

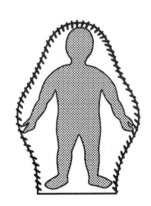

Remove pattern piece 1 C from the peach felt. Cover one side of the felt with fabric glue, and glue the felt piece on the puppet as shown in the diagram.

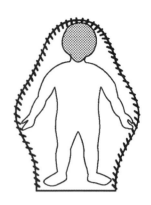

Attach pattern pieces 1 D and 1 E to the black felt, and cut out the felt. Remove the pattern pieces from the felt. Cover one side of the felt with fabric glue, and glue the felt pieces on the puppet as shown in the diagram.

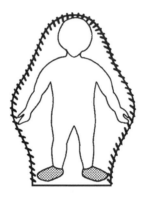

Attach pattern piece 16 B to the orange felt, and cut out the felt. Remove the pattern piece from the felt. Cover one side of the felt with fabric glue, and glue the felt piece on the puppet as shown in the diagram.

Attach pattern piece 16 A to the tan felt, and cut out the felt. Remove the pattern piece from the felt. Cover one side of the felt with fabric glue, and glue the felt piece on the puppet as shown in the diagram.

Attach pattern piece 6 A to the white felt, and cut out the felt. Remove the pattern piece from the felt. Cover one side of the felt with fabric glue, and glue the felt piece on the puppet as shown in the diagram.

Attach pattern piece 20 A to the gray felt, and cut out the felt. Remove the pattern piece from the felt. Cover one side of the felt with fabric glue, and glue the felt piece on the puppet as shown in the diagram. Add facial features and squiggles for words on stone tablets using three-dimensional fabric paint, permanent markers, or felt scraps.

Daniel

Possible Characters: Daniel, Wise Man, Disciple of Christ, the Samaritan in the story of the Good Samaritan, or any man in the Old or New Testament. Use a variety of felt colors and beard and head covering patterns to create multiple characters.

Materials:

- 2 light blue felt squares for puppet background

- Peach colored felt square for body and face

- Tan felt scraps for "under-tunic," head covering, and belt

- Blue felt square for robe and head covering

- Light brown felt scraps for hair and beard

- Black felt scraps for shoes

- Light blue embroidery thread

- Scissors

- Straight pins or masking tape

- Large tapestry needle, size 18 or 20

- Fabric glue

- Puppet Background A on page 133. Pattern pieces 1 A, 1 C, 1 D, and 1 E on page 136. Pattern pieces 6 B, 6 D, 6 F, 6 G, 6 H, and 6 I on page 141. Pattern pieces 14 B and 14 G on page 149. Pattern pieces 17 E and 17 F on page 152.

Directions:

Sew the puppet background according to the directions on page 9. Photocopy or trace the Daniel pattern pieces, and cut them out. Pin or tape the pattern pieces to the felt, and then cut out the felt. Rolled pieces of masking tape can be attached at several points to the back of each pattern piece. This will enable the pattern piece to stick to the felt while cutting. Follow the directions beside each diagram for cutting and gluing the pattern pieces. You may want to cut out all the felt pieces, and practice placing them on the puppet before gluing each piece in place.

Attach pattern pieces 1 A and 1 C to the peach felt, and cut out the felt. Remove pattern piece 1 A from the peach felt. Cover one side of the felt with fabric glue, and glue the felt piece on the puppet as shown in the diagram. Save pattern piece 1 C for the next step.

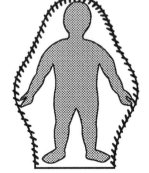

Easy-to-Make Bible Story Puppets

Remove pattern piece 1 C from the peach felt. Cover one side of the felt with fabric glue, and glue the felt piece on the puppet as shown in the diagram.

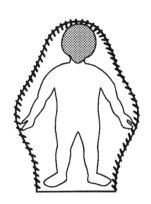

Attach pattern pieces 1 D and 1 E to the black felt, and cut out the felt. Remove the pattern pieces from the felt. Cover one side of the felt with fabric glue, and glue the felt pieces on the puppet as shown in the diagram.

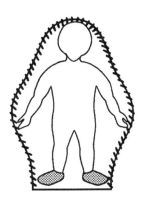

Attach pattern pieces 14 B and 14 G to the tan felt, and cut out the felt. Remove the pattern pieces from the felt. Cover one side of the felt with fabric glue, and glue the felt pieces on the puppet as shown in the diagram.

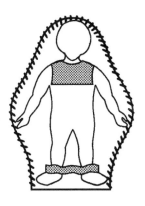

Attach pattern piece 17 F to the blue felt, and cut out the felt. Remove the pattern piece from the felt. Cover one side of the felt with fabric glue, and glue the felt piece on the puppet as shown in the diagram.

Attach pattern piece 17 E to the blue felt, and cut out the felt. Remove the pattern piece from the felt. Cover one side of the felt with fabric glue, and glue the felt piece on the puppet as shown in the diagram.

Attach pattern piece 6 H to the tan felt, and cut out the felt. Remove the pattern piece from the felt. Cover one side of the felt with fabric glue, and glue the felt piece on the puppet as shown in the diagram.

Attach pattern piece 6 I to the tan felt, and cut out the felt. Remove the pattern piece from the felt. Cover one side of the felt with fabric glue, and glue the felt piece on the puppet as shown in the diagram.

Attach pattern piece 6 B to the light brown felt, and cut out the felt. Remove the pattern piece from the felt. Cover one side of the felt with fabric glue, and glue the felt piece on the puppet as shown in the diagram.

Easy-to-Make Bible Story Puppets

Attach pattern piece 6 D to the tan felt, and cut out the felt. Remove the pattern piece from the felt. Cover one side of the felt with fabric glue, and glue the felt piece on the puppet as shown in the diagram.

Attach pattern piece 6 G to the blue felt, and cut out the felt. Remove the pattern piece from the felt. Cover one side of the felt with fabric glue, and glue the felt piece on the puppet as shown in the diagram.

Attach pattern piece 6 F to the blue felt, and cut out the felt. Remove the pattern piece from the felt. Cover one side of the felt with fabric glue, and glue the felt piece on the puppet as shown in the diagram. Add facial features using three-dimensional fabric paint, permanent markers, or felt scraps.

John the Baptist

Possible Characters: John the Baptist, Elijah, Esau, or the Israelite who was robbed and beaten in the story of the Good Samaritan.

Materials:

- 2 light blue felt squares for puppet background
- Peach colored felt square for body and face
- Brown felt scraps for animal skin garment
- Light brown felt scraps for hair and beard
- Black felt scraps for shoes
- Light blue embroidery thread
- Scissors
- Straight pins or masking tape
- Large tapestry needle, size 18 or 20
- Fabric glue
- Puppet Background A on page 133. Pattern pieces 1 A, 1 C, 1 D, and 1 E on page 136. Pattern pieces 6 A, and 6 K on page 141.

Directions:

Sew the puppet background according to the directions on page 9. Photocopy or trace the John the Baptist pattern pieces, and cut them out. Pin or tape the pattern pieces to the felt, and then cut out the felt. Rolled pieces of masking tape can be attached at several points to the back of each pattern piece. This will enable the pattern piece to stick to the felt while cutting. Follow the directions beside each diagram for cutting and gluing the pattern pieces. You may want to cut out all the felt pieces, and practice placing them on the puppet before gluing each piece in place.

Attach pattern pieces 1 A and 1 C to the peach felt, and cut out the felt. Remove pattern piece 1 A from the peach felt. Cover one side of the felt with fabric glue, and glue the felt piece on the puppet as shown in the diagram. Save pattern piece 1 C for the next step.

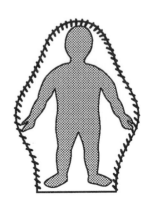

Easy-to-Make Bible Story Puppets

Remove pattern piece 1 C from the peach felt. Cover one side of the felt with fabric glue, and glue the felt piece on the puppet as shown in the diagram.

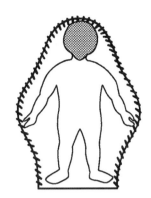

Attach pattern pieces 1 D and 1 E to the black felt, and cut out the felt. Remove the pattern pieces from the felt. Cover one side of the felt with fabric glue, and glue the felt pieces on the puppet as shown in the diagram.

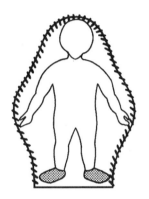

Attach pattern piece 6 A to the light brown felt, and cut out the felt. Remove the pattern piece from the felt. Cover one side of the felt with fabric glue, and glue the felt piece on the puppet as shown in the diagram.

Attach pattern piece 6 K to the brown felt, and cut out the felt. Remove the pattern piece from the felt. Cover one side of the felt with fabric glue, and glue the felt piece on the puppet as shown in the diagram.

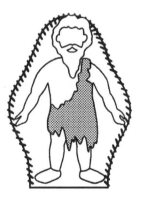

Add facial features using three-dimensional fabric paint, permanent markers, or felt scraps.

Shepherd

Possible Characters: Shepherd, Disciple of Jesus, Wise Man, Jesus, or any of Joseph's brothers in the story of Joseph and his Coat of many Colors. Use a variety of felt colors and beard and head covering patterns to produce multiple characters. Omit staff or outer robe if desired.

Materials:

- 2 light blue felt squares for puppet background
- Peach colored felt square for body and face
- Yellow felt square for tunic
- Green felt square for robe and headband
- Brown felt scraps for hair, beard, and staff
- Black felt scraps for shoes
- Light blue embroidery thread
- Scissors
- Straight pins or masking tape
- Large tapestry needle, size 18 or 20
- Fabric glue
- Puppet Background A on page 133. Pattern pieces 1 A, 1 C, 1 D, and 1 E on page 136. Pattern pieces 6 C, 6 H, 6 J, and 6 L on page 141. Pattern pieces 14 A, 14 E, and 14 F on page 149. Pattern piece 17 A on page 152.

Directions:

Sew the puppet background according to the directions on page 9. Photocopy or trace the Shepherd pattern pieces, and cut them out. Pin or tape the pattern pieces to the felt, and then cut out the felt. Rolled pieces of masking tape can be attached at several points to the back of each pattern piece. This will enable the pattern piece to stick to the felt while cutting. Follow the directions beside each diagram for cutting and gluing the pattern pieces. You may want to cut out all the felt pieces, and practice placing them on the puppet before gluing each piece in place.

Attach pattern pieces 1 A and 1 C to the peach felt, and cut out the felt. Remove pattern piece 1 A from the peach felt. Cover one side of the felt with fabric glue, and glue the felt piece on the puppet as shown in the diagram. Save pattern piece 1 C for the next step.

Easy-to-Make Bible Story Puppets

Remove pattern piece 1 C from the peach felt. Cover one side of the felt with fabric glue, and glue the felt piece on the puppet as shown in the diagram.

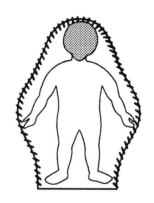

Attach pattern pieces 1 D and 1 E to the black felt, and cut out the felt. Remove the pattern pieces from the felt. Cover one side of the felt with fabric glue, and glue the felt pieces on the puppet as shown in the diagram.

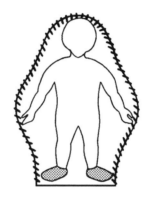

Attach pattern piece 14 A to the yellow felt, and cut out the felt. Remove the pattern piece from the felt. Cover one side of the felt with fabric glue, and glue the felt piece on the puppet as shown in the diagram.

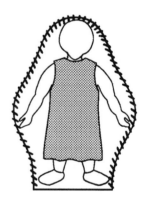

Attach pattern piece 6 H to the green felt, and cut out the felt. Remove the pattern piece from the felt. Cover one side of the felt with fabric glue, and glue the felt piece on the puppet as shown in the diagram.

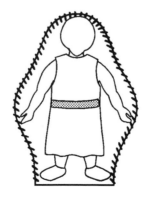

Attach pattern pieces 14 E and 14 F to the green felt, and cut out the felt. Remove the pattern pieces from the felt. Cover one side of the felt with fabric glue, and glue the felt pieces on the puppet as shown in the diagram.

Attach pattern piece 6 C to the brown felt, and cut out the felt. Remove the pattern piece from the felt. Cover one side of the felt with fabric glue, and glue the felt piece on the puppet as shown in the diagram.

Attach pattern piece 6 J to the green felt, and cut out the felt. Remove the pattern piece from the felt. Cover one side of the felt with fabric glue, and glue the felt piece on the puppet as shown in the diagram.

Attach pattern piece 6 L to the green felt, and cut out the felt. Remove the pattern piece from the felt. Cover one side of the felt with fabric glue, and glue the felt piece on the puppet as shown in the diagram.

Attach pattern piece 17 A to the brown felt, and cut out the felt. Remove the pattern piece from the felt. Cover one side of the felt with fabric glue, and glue the felt piece on the puppet as shown in the diagram. Add facial features using three-dimensional fabric paint, permanent markers, or felt scraps.

Boy

Possible Characters: Boy in the story of the Loaves and Fishes; boy from when the Messiah says, "Suffer the little children to come unto me and forbid them not"; Benjamin in the story of Joseph and his Coat of many Colors; Isaac as a child; Aaron as a child in the story of Baby Moses; Samuel as a boy; any boy in the Old or New Testament.

Materials:

- 2 light blue felt squares for puppet background
- Peach colored felt square for body and face
- Tan felt for belt and head covering
- Red felt square for tunic and head covering
- Brown felt scraps for hair
- Black felt scraps for shoes
- Light blue embroidery thread
- Scissors
- Straight pins or masking tape
- Large tapestry needle, size 18 or 20
- Fabric glue
- Puppet Background A on page 133. Pattern pieces 3 A, 3 B, 3 C, 3 D, 3 F, 3 H, 3 I, and 3 J on page 138. Pattern piece 13 C on page 148.

Directions:

Sew the puppet background according to the directions on page 9. Photocopy or trace the Boy pattern pieces, and cut them out. Pin or tape the pattern pieces to the felt, and then cut out the felt. Rolled pieces of masking tape can be attached at several points to the back of each pattern piece. This will enable the pattern piece to stick to the felt while cutting. Follow the directions beside each diagram for cutting and gluing the pattern pieces. You may want to cut out all the felt pieces, and practice placing them on the puppet before gluing each piece in place.

Attach pattern pieces 3 A and 3 H to the peach felt, and cut out the felt. Remove pattern piece 3 A from the peach felt. Cover one side of the felt with fabric glue, and glue the felt piece on the puppet as shown in the diagram. Save pattern piece 3 H for the next step.

Remove pattern piece 3 H from the peach felt. Cover one side of the felt with fabric glue, and glue the felt piece on the puppet as shown in the diagram.

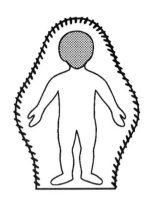

Attach pattern piece 3 B to the brown felt, and cut out the felt. Remove the pattern piece from the felt. Cover one side of the felt with fabric glue, and glue the felt piece on the puppet as shown in the diagram.

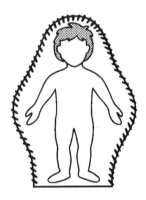

Attach pattern piece 3 C to the red felt, and cut out the felt. Remove the pattern piece from the felt. Cover one side of the felt with fabric glue, and glue the felt piece on the puppet as shown in the diagram.

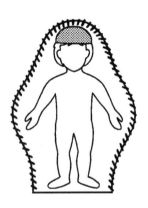

Attach pattern piece 3 D to the tan felt, and cut out the felt. Remove the pattern piece from the felt. Cover one side of the felt with fabric glue, and glue the felt piece on the puppet as shown in the diagram.

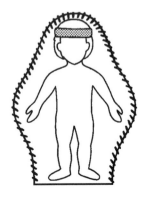

Easy-to-Make Bible Story Puppets

Attach pattern piece 13 C to the red felt, and cut out the felt. Remove the pattern piece from the felt. Cover one side of the felt with fabric glue, and glue the felt piece on the puppet as shown in the diagram.

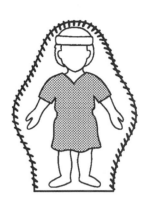

Attach pattern piece 3 F to the tan felt, and cut out the felt. Remove the pattern piece from the felt. Cover one side of the felt with fabric glue, and glue the felt piece on the puppet as shown in the diagram.

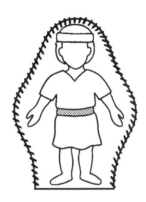

Attach pattern pieces 3 I and 3 J to the black felt, and cut out the felt. Remove the pattern pieces from the felt. Cover one side of the felt with fabric glue, and glue the felt pieces on the puppet as shown in the diagram.

Add facial features using three-dimensional fabric paint, permanent markers, or felt scraps.

The Boy David

Materials:

- 2 light blue felt squares for puppet background
- Peach colored felt square for body and face
- Tan felt for headband
- Orange felt scraps for tunic
- Brown felt scraps for hair
- Black felt scraps for shoes and sling
- White felt for stones
- Light blue embroidery thread
- Scissors
- Straight pins or masking tape
- Large tapestry needle, size 18 or 20
- Fabric glue
- Puppet Background A on page 133. Pattern pieces 3 A, 3 B, 3 E, 3 G, 3 H, 3 I, 3 J, 3 K, and 3 L on page 138. Pattern piece 13 D on page 148.

Directions:

Sew the puppet background according to the directions on page 9. Photocopy or trace the Boy David pattern pieces, and cut them out. Pin or tape the pattern pieces to the felt, and then cut out the felt. Rolled pieces of masking tape can be attached at several points to the back of each pattern piece. This will enable the pattern piece to stick to the felt while cutting. Follow the directions beside each diagram for cutting and gluing the pattern pieces. You may want to cut out all the felt pieces, and practice placing them on the puppet before gluing each piece in place.

Attach pattern pieces 3 A and 3 H to the peach felt, and cut out the felt. Remove pattern piece 3 A from the peach felt. Cover one side of the felt with fabric glue, and glue the felt piece on the puppet as shown in the diagram. Save pattern piece 3 H for the next step.

Remove pattern piece 3 H from the peach felt. Cover one side of the felt with fabric glue, and glue the felt piece on the puppet as shown in the diagram.

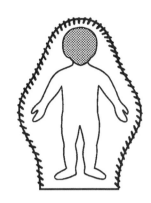

Attach pattern piece 3 B to the brown felt, and cut out the felt. Remove the pattern piece from the felt. Cover one side of the felt with fabric glue, and glue the felt piece on the puppet as shown in the diagram.

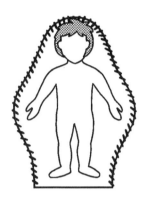

Attach pattern piece 3 E to the tan felt, and cut out the felt. Remove the pattern piece from the felt. Cover one side of the felt with fabric glue, and glue the felt piece on the puppet as shown in the diagram.

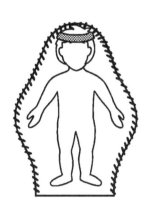

Attach pattern piece 13 D to the orange felt, and cut out the felt. Remove the pattern piece from the felt. Cover one side of the felt with fabric glue, and glue the felt piece on the puppet as shown in the diagram.

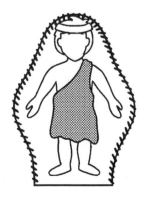

Attach pattern pieces 3 I and 3 J to the black felt, and cut out the felt. Remove the pattern pieces from the felt. Cover one side of the felt with fabric glue, and glue the felt pieces on the puppet as shown in the diagram.

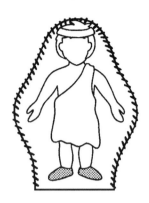

Attach pattern piece 3 K to the black felt, and attach pattern pieces labeled 3 L to the white felt, and cut out the felt. Remove the pattern pieces from the felt. Cover one side of the felt with fabric glue, and glue the felt pieces on the puppet as shown in the diagram.

Attach pattern piece 3 G to the black felt, and cut out the felt. Remove the pattern piece from the felt. Cover one side of the felt with fabric glue, and glue the felt piece on the puppet as shown in the diagram. Add facial features using three-dimensional fabric paint, permanent markers, or felt scraps.

The Prodigal Son

Possible Characters: The Prodigal Son after he lost all his money or a shepherd boy.

Materials:

- 2 light blue felt squares for puppet background

- Peach colored felt square for body and face

- Brown felt for headband

- Brown felt scraps for tunic

- Tan felt scraps for hair

- Black felt scraps for shoes

- Light blue embroidery thread

- Scissors

- Straight pins or masking tape

- Large tapestry needle, size 18 or 20

- Fabric glue

- Puppet Background A on page 133. Pattern pieces 3 A, 3 B, 3 E, 3 H, 3 I, and 3 J on page 138. Pattern piece 13 D on page 148.

Directions:

Sew the puppet background according to the directions on page 9. Photocopy or trace The Prodigal Son pattern pieces, and cut them out. Pin or tape the pattern pieces to the felt, and then cut out the felt. Rolled pieces of masking tape can be attached at several points to the back of each pattern piece. This will enable the pattern piece to stick to the felt while cutting. Follow the directions beside each diagram for cutting and gluing the pattern pieces. You may want to cut out all the felt pieces, and practice placing them on the puppet before gluing each piece in place.

Attach pattern pieces 3 A and 3 H to the peach felt, and cut out the felt. Remove pattern piece 3 A from the peach felt. Cover one side of the felt with fabric glue, and glue the felt piece on the puppet as shown in the diagram. Save pattern piece 3 H for the next step.

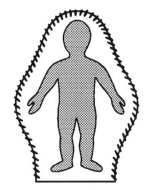

Remove pattern piece 3 H from the peach felt. Cover one side of the felt with fabric glue, and glue the felt piece on the puppet as shown in the diagram.

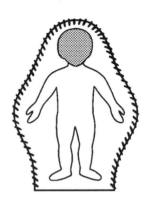

Attach pattern piece 3 B to the tan felt, and cut out the felt. Remove the pattern piece from the felt. Cover one side of the felt with fabric glue, and glue the felt piece on the puppet as shown in the diagram.

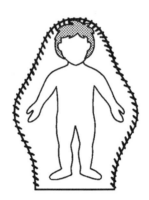

Attach pattern piece 3 E to the brown felt, and cut out the felt. Remove the pattern piece from the felt. Cover one side of the felt with fabric glue, and glue the felt piece on the puppet as shown in the diagram.

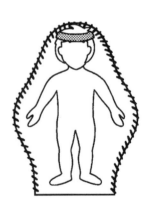

Attach pattern piece 13 D to the brown felt, and cut out the felt. Remove the pattern piece from the felt. Cover one side of the felt with fabric glue, and glue the felt piece on the puppet as shown in the diagram.

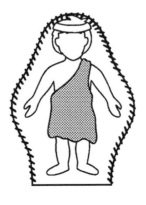

Easy-to-Make Bible Story Puppets

Attach pattern pieces 3 I and 3 J to the black felt, and cut out the felt. Remove the pattern pieces from the felt. Cover one side of the felt with fabric glue, and glue the felt pieces on the puppet as shown in the diagram.

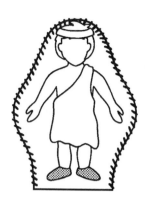

Add facial features using three-dimensional fabric paint, permanent markers, or felt scraps.

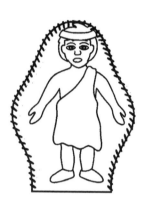

Joseph and His Coat of Many Colors

Possible Characters: Joseph, The Prodigal Son when his father welcomes him home and puts a coat on him, or any boy in the Old or New Testament.

Materials:

- 2 light blue felt squares for puppet background
- Peach colored felt square for body and face
- Medium blue felt for head covering and robe
- Yellow felt scraps for headband and belt
- Green felt scraps for tunic
- Green and yellow felt scraps for stripes on robe or green and yellow yarn
- Brown felt scraps for hair
- Black felt scraps for shoes
- Light blue embroidery thread
- Scissors
- Straight pins or masking tape
- Large tapestry needle, size 18 or 20
- Fabric glue
- Puppet Background A on page 133. Pattern pieces 3 A, 3 B, 3 C, 3 D, 3 F, 3 H, 3 I, and 3 J on page 138. Pattern pieces 13 A, 13 B, and 13 C on page 148.

Directions:

Sew the puppet background according to the directions on page 9. Photocopy or trace the Joseph and His Coat of Many Colors pattern pieces, and cut them out. Pin or tape the pattern pieces to the felt, and then cut out the felt. Rolled pieces of masking tape can be attached at several points to the back of each pattern piece. This will enable the pattern piece to stick to the felt while cutting. Follow the directions beside each diagram for cutting and gluing the pattern pieces. You may want to cut out all the felt pieces, and practice placing them on the puppet before gluing each piece in place.

Attach pattern pieces 3 A and 3 H to the peach felt, and cut out the felt. Remove pattern piece 3 A from the peach felt. Cover one side of the felt with fabric glue, and glue the felt piece on the puppet as shown in the diagram. Save pattern piece 3 H for the next step.

Easy-to-Make Bible Story Puppets

Remove pattern piece 3 H from the peach felt. Cover one side of the felt with fabric glue, and glue the felt piece on the puppet as shown in the diagram.

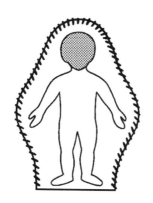

Attach pattern piece 3 B to the brown felt, and cut out the felt. Remove the pattern piece from the felt. Cover one side of the felt with fabric glue, and glue the felt piece on the puppet as shown in the diagram.

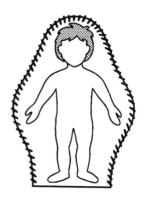

Attach pattern piece 3 C to the medium blue felt, and cut out the felt. Remove the pattern piece from the felt. Cover one side of the felt with fabric glue, and glue the felt piece on the puppet as shown in the diagram.

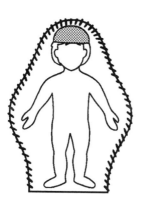

Attach pattern piece 3 D to the yellow felt, and cut out the felt. Remove the pattern piece from the felt. Cover one side of the felt with fabric glue, and glue the felt piece on the puppet as shown in the diagram.

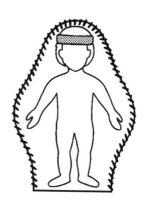

Attach pattern piece 13 C to the green felt, and cut out the felt. Remove the pattern piece from the felt. Cover one side of the felt with fabric glue, and glue the felt piece on the puppet as shown in the diagram.

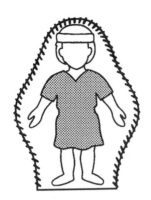

Attach pattern piece 3 F to the yellow felt, and cut out the felt. Remove the pattern piece from the felt. Cover one side of the felt with fabric glue, and glue the felt piece on the puppet as shown in the diagram.

Attach pattern pieces 3 I and 3 J to the black felt, and cut out the felt. Remove the pattern pieces from the felt. Cover one side of the felt with fabric glue, and glue the felt pieces on the puppet as shown in the diagram.

Attach pattern pieces 13 A and 13 B to the medium blue felt, and cut out the felt. Remove the pattern pieces from the felt. Cover one side of the felt with fabric glue, and glue the felt pieces on the puppet as shown in the diagram.

Cut strips of yellow and green felt and glue them to the robe to create stripes, or glue on pieces of yellow and green yarn. Add facial features using three-dimensional fabric paint, permanent markers, or felt scraps.

Easy-to-Make Bible Story Puppets

Adam

Materials:

- 2 light blue felt squares for puppet background

- Peach colored felt square for body and face

- Green felt square for leaf garment

- Brown felt square for animal skin garment (optional)

- Brown felt scraps hair

- Light blue embroidery thread

- Scissors

- Straight pins or masking tape

- Large tapestry needle, size 18 or 20

- Fabric glue

- Puppet Background A on page 133. Pattern pieces 1 A, 1 B, and 1 C on page 136. Pattern piece 10 A on page 145.

Directions:

Sew the puppet background according to the directions on page 9. Photocopy or trace the Adam pattern pieces, and cut them out. Pin or tape the pattern pieces to the felt, and then cut out the felt. Rolled pieces of masking tape can be attached at several points to the back of each pattern piece. This will enable the pattern piece to stick to the felt while cutting. Follow the directions beside each diagram for cutting and gluing the pattern pieces. You may want to cut out all the felt pieces, and practice placing them on the puppet before gluing each piece in place.

Attach pattern pieces 1 A and 1 C to the peach felt, and cut out the felt. Remove pattern piece 1 A from the peach felt. Cover one side of the felt with fabric glue, and glue the felt piece on the puppet as shown in the diagram. Save pattern piece 1 C for the next step.

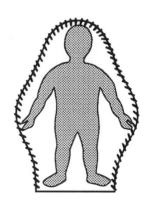

Remove pattern piece 1 C from the peach felt. Cover one side of the felt with fabric glue, and glue the felt piece on the puppet as shown in the diagram.

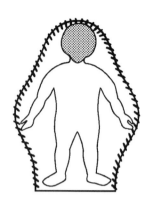

Attach pattern piece 1 B to the brown felt, and cut out the felt. Remove the pattern piece from the felt. Cover one side of the felt with fabric glue, and glue the felt piece on the puppet as shown in the diagram.

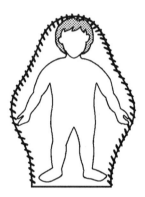

Attach pattern piece 10 A to the green felt, and cut out the felt. Remove the pattern piece from the felt. Cover one side of the felt with fabric glue, and glue the felt piece on the puppet as shown in the diagram. (You may choose to make an animal skin garment using the same pattern cut from brown felt. This can be placed over the leaf garment to indicate when the Lord made clothes for Adam and Eve out of animal skins. This does not need to be glued on, but can simply be added by attaching a piece of rolled masking tape to the back of the brown felt piece.)

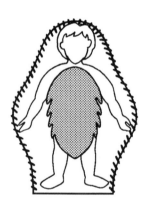

Add facial features and lines for leaf veins using three-dimensional fabric paint, permanent markers, yarn, or felt scraps.

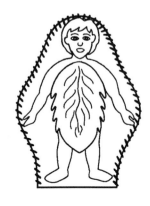

Easy-to-Make Bible Story Puppets

Roman Soldier

Materials:

- 2 light blue felt squares for puppet background

- Peach colored felt square for body and face

- Gray felt square for armor, shield, helmet, and spear tip

- Red felt square for tunic and helmet tip

- Brown felt scraps for hair, shield emblems, and spear

- Black felt scraps for shoes

- Light blue embroidery thread

- Scissors

- Straight pins or masking tape

- Large tapestry needle, size 18 or 20

- Fabric glue

- Puppet Background A on page 133. Pattern pieces 1 A, 1 B, 1 C, 1 D, and 1 E on page 136. Pattern pieces 18 A, 18 B, 18 C, 18 D, 18 E, 18 F, 18 G, 18 H, and 18 K on page 153. Pattern pieces 20 D, 20 E, 20 F, 20 G, 20 H, 20 I, and 20 J on page 155.

Directions:

Sew the puppet background according to the directions on page 9. Photocopy or trace the Roman Soldier pattern pieces, and cut them out. Pin or tape the pattern pieces to the felt, and then cut out the felt. Rolled pieces of masking tape can be attached at several points to the back of each pattern piece. This will enable the pattern piece to stick to the felt while cutting. Follow the directions beside each diagram for cutting and gluing the pattern pieces. You may want to cut out all the felt pieces, and practice placing them on the puppet before gluing each piece in place.

Attach pattern pieces 1 A and 1 C to the peach felt, and cut out the felt. Remove pattern piece 1 A from the peach felt. Cover one side of the felt with fabric glue, and glue the felt piece on the puppet as shown in the diagram. Save pattern piece 1 C for the next step.

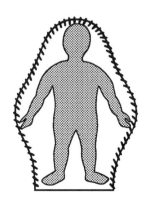

Remove pattern piece 1 C from the peach felt. Cover one side of the felt with fabric glue, and glue the felt piece on the puppet as shown in the diagram.

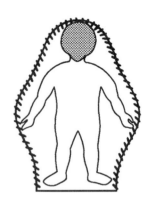

Attach pattern piece 1 B to the brown felt, and cut out the felt. Remove the pattern piece from the felt. Cover one side of the felt with fabric glue, and glue the felt piece on the puppet as shown in the diagram.

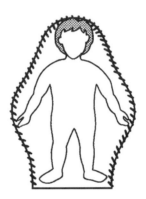

Attach pattern piece 18 K to the gray felt, and cut out the felt. Remove the pattern piece from the felt. Cover one side of the felt with fabric glue, and glue the felt piece on the puppet as shown in the diagram.

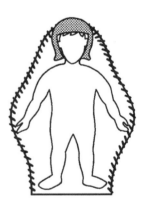

Attach pattern piece 18 G to the gray felt, and cut out the felt. Remove the pattern piece from the felt. Cover one side of the felt with fabric glue, and glue the felt piece on the puppet as shown in the diagram.

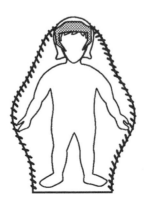

Easy-to-Make Bible Story Puppets

Attach pattern piece 18 H to the red felt, and cut out the felt. Attach pattern pieces 1 D and 1 E to the black felt, and cut out the felt. Remove the pattern pieces from the felt. Cover one side of the felt with fabric glue, and glue the felt pieces on the puppet as shown in the diagram.

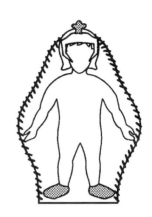

Attach pattern piece 18 A to the red felt, and cut out the felt. Remove the pattern piece from the felt. Cover one side of the felt with fabric glue, and glue the felt piece on the puppet as shown in the diagram.

Attach pattern piece 18 F to the gray felt, and cut out the felt. Remove the pattern piece from the felt. Cover one side of the felt with fabric glue, and glue the felt piece on the puppet as shown in the diagram.

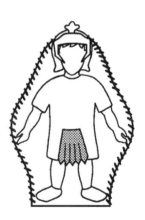

Attach pattern piece 18 C to the gray felt, and cut out the felt. Remove the pattern piece from the felt. Cover one side of the felt with fabric glue, and glue the felt piece on the puppet as shown in the diagram.

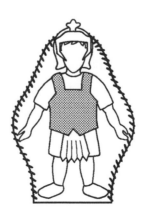

Attach the pattern pieces labeled 18 B to the brown felt, and cut out the felt. Attach pattern pieces 18 D and 18 E to the gray felt, and cut out the felt. Remove the pattern pieces from the felt. Cover one side of the felt with fabric glue, and glue the felt pieces on the puppet as shown in the diagram.

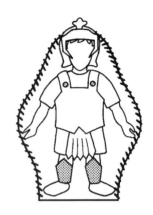

Attach pattern piece 20 D to the gray felt, and cut out the felt. Attach pattern piece 20 F to the brown felt, and cut out the felt. Remove the pattern pieces from the felt. Cover one side of the felt with fabric glue, and glue the felt pieces on the puppet as shown in the diagram.

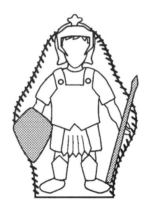

Attach pattern piece 20 E to the gray felt, and cut out the felt. Attach pattern piece 20 G to the brown felt, and cut out the felt. Remove the pattern pieces from the felt. Cover one side of the felt with fabric glue, and glue the felt pieces on the puppet as shown in the diagram.

Attach pattern piece 20 H to the gray felt, and cut out the felt. Attach pattern pieces labeled 20 J to the brown felt, and cut out the felt. Remove the pattern pieces from the felt. Cover one side of the felt with fabric glue, and glue the felt pieces on the puppet as shown in the diagram.

Attach pattern piece 20 I to the brown felt, and cut out the felt. Remove the pattern piece from the felt. Cover one side of the felt with fabric glue, and glue the felt piece on the puppet as shown in the diagram. Add facial features using three-dimensional fabric paint, permanent markers, or felt scraps.

Easy-to-Make Bible Story Puppets

Egyptian Man

Possible Characters: Potifer, Joseph as Pharaoh's right-hand man, or any Egyptian nobleman or prince.

Materials:

- 2 light blue felt squares for puppet background

- Tan colored felt square for body and face

- Yellow felt square for kilt, collar, armbands, head covering, and sash

- Medium blue felt scraps for collar, head covering, and sash

- Light blue embroidery thread

- Scissors

- Straight pins or masking tape

- Large tapestry needle, size 18 or 20

- Fabric glue

- Puppet Background A on page 133. Pattern piece 1 A and 1 C on page 136. Pattern pieces 19 A, 19 B, 19 C, 19 D, 19 E, 19 F, 19 G, 19 H, 19 I, 19 J, 19 M, and 19 N on page 154.

Directions:

Sew the puppet background according to the directions on page 9. Photocopy or trace the Egyptian Man pattern pieces, and cut them out. Pin or tape the pattern pieces to the felt, and then cut out the felt. Rolled pieces of masking tape can be attached at several points to the back of each pattern piece. This will enable the pattern piece to stick to the felt while cutting. Follow the directions beside each diagram for cutting and gluing the pattern pieces. You may want to cut out all the felt pieces, and practice placing them on the puppet before gluing each piece in place.

Attach pattern pieces 1 A and 1 C to the tan felt, and cut out the felt. Remove the pattern pieces from the tan felt. Cover one side of the felt with fabric glue, and glue the felt pieces on the puppet as shown in the diagram. Save pattern piece 1 C for later.

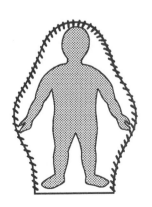

Attach pattern piece 19 B to the yellow felt, and cut out the felt. Remove the pattern piece from the felt. Cover one side of the felt with fabric glue, and glue the felt piece on the puppet as shown in the diagram.

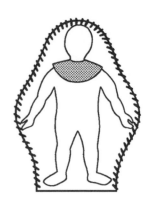

Remove pattern piece 1 C from the tan felt. Cover one side of the felt with fabric glue, and glue the felt piece on the puppet as shown in the diagram.

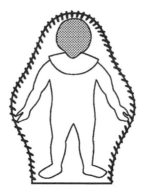

Attach pattern piece 19 M to the medium blue felt, and cut out the felt. Remove the pattern piece from the felt. Cover one side of the felt with fabric glue, and glue the felt piece on the puppet as shown in the diagram.

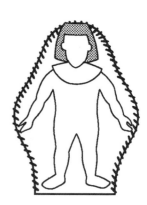

Attach pattern piece 19 N to the yellow felt, and cut out the felt. Remove the pattern piece from the felt. Cover one side of the felt with fabric glue, and glue the felt piece on the puppet as shown in the diagram.

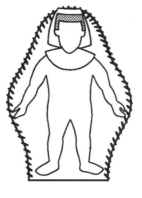

Attach pattern piece 19 E to the medium blue felt, and cut out the felt. Attach pieces 19 G, 19 H, 19 I, and 19 J to the yellow felt, and cut out the felt. Remove the pattern pieces from the felt. Cover one side of the felt with fabric glue, and glue the felt pieces on the puppet as shown in the diagram.

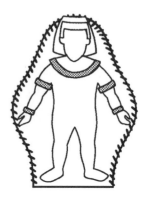

Attach pattern piece 19 A to the yellow felt, and cut out the felt. Remove the pattern piece from the felt. Cover one side of the felt with fabric glue, and glue the felt piece on the puppet as shown in the diagram.

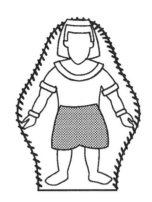

Attach pattern piece 19 F to the medium blue felt, and cut out the felt. Remove the pattern piece from the felt. Cover one side of the felt with fabric glue, and glue the felt piece on the puppet as shown in the diagram.

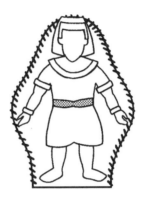

Attach pattern piece 19 C to the yellow felt, and cut out the felt. Remove the pattern piece from the felt. Cover one side of the felt with fabric glue, and glue the felt piece on the puppet as shown in the diagram.

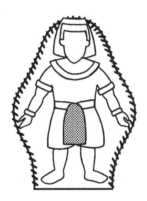

Attach pattern piece 19 D to the medium blue felt, and cut out the felt. Remove the pattern piece from the felt. Cover one side of the felt with fabric glue, and glue the felt piece on the puppet as shown in the diagram.

Add facial features using three-dimensional fabric paint, permanent markers, or felt scraps.

Goliath

Materials:

- 2 light blue felt squares for puppet background
- Peach colored felt square for body and face
- Dark brown felt square for tunic
- Medium brown felt scraps for spear and shield
- Tan felt scraps for spear tip and shield
- Gray felt square for armor, and helmet
- Red felt scrap for helmet tip
- Black felt scraps for beard, and shoes
- Light blue embroidery thread
- Scissors
- Straight pins or masking tape
- Large tapestry needle, size 18 or 20
- Fabric glue
- Puppet Background A on page 133. Pattern pieces 21 A, 21 B and 21 C on page 156. Pattern pieces 22 A through 22 H on page 157. Pattern pieces 23 A through 23 K on page 158.

Directions:

Cut out two pieces of light blue felt using Puppet Background A found on page 133, but do not sew the pieces together yet. Cut out two pieces of light blue felt using pattern piece 22 G. Apply glue to both felt pieces cut from pattern piece 22 G as indicated on pattern. Adhere each 22 G felt piece to each Puppet Background A felt piece as shown in the diagram # 1. This expands the Puppet Background to accommodate Goliath's large size. Next place both Puppet Background felt pieces together and sew outer edges as shown in diagram #2. (See page 9 for sewing directions.)

Diagram #1

Photocopy or trace the Goliath pattern pieces, and cut them out. Pin or tape the pattern pieces to the felt, and then cut out the felt. Rolled pieces of masking tape can be attached at several points to the back of each pattern piece. This will enable the pattern piece to stick to the felt while cutting. Follow the directions beside each diagram for cutting and gluing the pattern pieces. You may want to cut out all the felt pieces, and practice placing them on the puppet before gluing each piece in place.

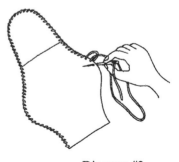

Diagram #2

Attach pattern pieces 21 A and 21 C to the peach felt, and cut out the felt. Remove pattern piece 21 A from the peach felt. Cover one side of the felt with fabric glue, and glue the felt piece on the puppet as shown in the diagram. Save pattern piece 21 C for later.

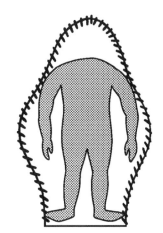

Attach pattern piece 23 J to the gray felt, and cut out the felt. Remove the pattern piece from the felt. Cover one side of the felt with fabric glue, and glue the felt piece on the puppet as shown in the diagram.

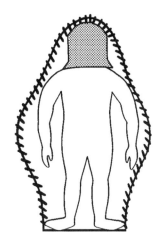

Attach pattern piece 22 A to the brown felt, and cut out the felt. Remove the pattern piece from the felt. Cover one side of the felt with fabric glue, and glue the felt piece on the puppet as shown in the diagram.

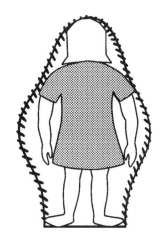

Remove pattern piece 21 C from the peach felt. Cover one side of the felt with fabric glue, and glue the felt piece on the puppet as shown in the diagram.

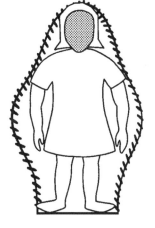

Attach pattern piece 21 B to the black felt, and cut out the felt. Remove the pattern piece from the felt. Cover one side of the felt with fabric glue, and glue the felt piece on the puppet as shown in the diagram.

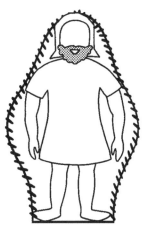

Attach pattern piece 23 H to the gray felt, and cut out the felt. Remove the pattern piece from the felt. Cover one side of the felt with fabric glue, and glue the felt piece on the puppet as shown in the diagram.

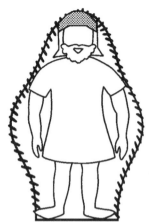

Attach pattern piece 23 E to the gray felt, and cut out the felt. Remove the pattern piece from the felt. Cover one side of the felt with fabric glue, and glue the felt piece on the puppet as shown in the diagram.

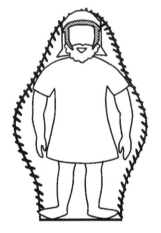

Attach pattern piece 22 C to the red felt, and cut out the felt. Remove the pattern piece from the felt. Cover one side of the felt with fabric glue, and glue the felt piece on the puppet as shown in the diagram.

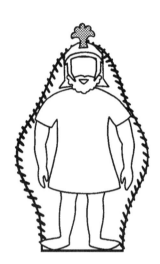

Attach pattern piece 23 D to the gray felt, and cut out the felt. Remove the pattern piece from the felt. Cover one side of the felt with fabric glue, and glue the felt piece on the puppet as shown in the diagram.

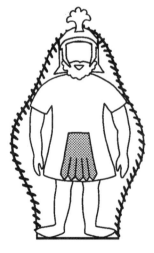

Attach pattern piece 23 I to the gray felt, and cut out the felt. Remove the pattern piece from the felt. Cover one side of the felt with fabric glue, and glue the felt piece on the puppet as shown in the diagram.

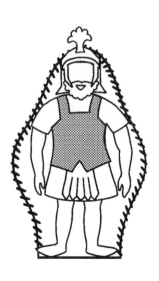

Attach pattern pieces 23 B and 23 C to the black felt, and cut out the felt. Remove the pattern pieces from the felt. Cover one side of the felt with fabric glue, and glue the felt pieces on the puppet as shown in the diagram.

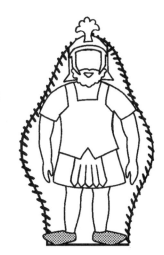

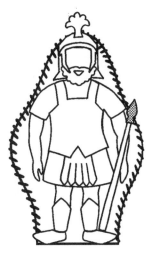

Attach pattern pieces 23 F and 23 G to the gray felt, and cut out the felt. Remove the pattern pieces from the felt. Cover one side of the felt with fabric glue, and glue the felt pieces on the puppet as shown in the diagram.

Attach pattern pieces 22 B to the medium brown felt, and cut out the felt. Remove the pattern piece from the felt. Cover one side of the felt with fabric glue, and glue the felt piece on the puppet as shown in the diagram.

Attach pattern piece 22 F to the tan felt, and cut out the felt. Remove the pattern piece from the felt. Cover one side of the felt with fabric glue, and glue the felt piece on the puppet as shown in the diagram.

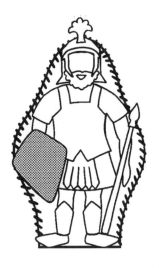

Attach pattern pieces 23 A to the medium brown felt, and cut out the felt. Remove the pattern piece from the felt. Cover one side of the felt with fabric glue, and glue the felt piece on the puppet as shown in the diagram.

Attach pattern piece 22 H to the tan felt, and cut out the felt. Remove the pattern piece from the felt. Cover one side of the felt with fabric glue, and glue the felt piece on the puppet as shown in the diagram.

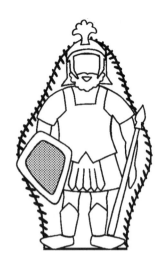

Attach pattern piece 22 E to the medium brown felt, and cut out the felt. Remove the pattern piece from the felt. Cover one side of the felt with fabric glue, and glue the felt piece on the puppet as shown in the diagram.

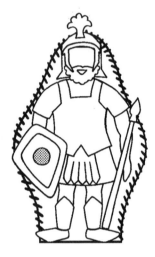

Attach pattern pieces labeled 22 D to the tan felt, and cut out the felt. Remove the pattern pieces from the felt. Cover one side of the felt with fabric glue, and glue the felt pieces on the puppet as shown in the diagram.

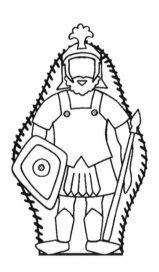

Add facial features using three-dimensional fabric paint, permanent markers, or felt scraps.

King

Possible Characters: King Ahasuerus in the story of Esther, King Darius in the story of Daniel in the Lion's Den, King Saul, King Solomon, King Herod, or any king in the Old or New Testaments. (See page 96 for Pharaoh.)

Materials:

- 2 light blue felt squares for puppet background
- Peach colored felt square for body and face
- Red felt square for tunic, robe trimming, and jewels
- Purple felt square for robe
- Yellow felt scraps for crown, collar, and belt
- Brown felt scraps for hair and beard
- Black felt scraps for shoes
- Light blue embroidery thread
- Scissors
- Straight pins or masking tape
- Large tapestry needle, size 18 or 20
- Fabric glue
- Puppet Background A on page 133. Pattern pieces 1 A, 1 C, 1 D, and 1 E on page 136. Pattern pieces 6 B and 6 H on page 141. Pattern pieces 15 C, 15 D, 15 E, 15 F, 15 G, and 15 H on page 150. Pattern piece 16 B on page 151. Pattern pieces 18 I, 18 J, 18 L, 18 M and 18 N on page 153.

Directions:

Sew the puppet background according to the directions on page 9. Photocopy or trace the King pattern pieces, and cut them out. Pin or tape the pattern pieces to the felt, and then cut out the felt. Rolled pieces of masking tape can be attached at several points to the back of each pattern piece. This will enable the pattern piece to stick to the felt while cutting. Follow the directions beside each diagram for cutting and gluing the pattern pieces. You may want to cut out all the felt pieces, and practice placing them on the puppet before gluing each piece in place.

Attach pattern pieces 1 A and 1 C to the peach felt, and cut out the felt. Remove pattern piece 1 A from the peach felt. Cover one side of the felt with fabric glue, and glue the felt piece on the puppet as shown in the diagram. Save pattern piece 1 C for later.

Attach pattern pieces 1 D and 1 E to the
black felt, and cut out the felt. Remove the
pattern pieces from the felt. Cover one side
of the felt with fabric glue, and glue the felt
pieces on the puppet as shown in the
diagram.

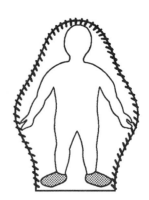

Attach pattern piece 16 B to the red felt,
and cut out the felt. Remove the pattern
piece from the felt. Cover one side of the
felt with fabric glue, and glue the felt piece
on the puppet as shown in the diagram.

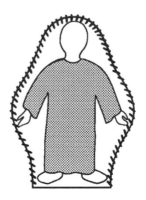

Attach pattern piece 18 L to the yellow felt, and cut out
the felt. Attach pattern piece 6 H to the purple felt, and
cut out the felt. Remove the pattern pieces from the
felt. Cover one side of the felt with fabric glue, and glue
the felt pieces on the puppet as shown in the diagram.

Attach pattern pieces 15 D and 15 G to the
purple felt, and cut out the felt. Remove the
pattern pieces from the felt. Cover one side
of the felt with fabric glue, and glue the felt
pieces on the puppet as shown in the
diagram.

Attach pattern pieces 15 C, 15 E, 15 F, and
15 H to the red felt, and cut out the felt.
Remove the pattern pieces from the felt.
Cover one side of the felt with fabric glue,
and glue the felt pieces on the puppet as
shown in the diagram.

Easy-to-Make Bible Story Puppets

Attach pattern piece 18 J and pattern piece 18 N to the red felt, and cut out the felt. Remove the pattern pieces from the felt. Cover one side of the felt with fabric glue, and glue the felt pieces on the puppet as shown in the diagram.

Remove pattern piece 1 C from the peach felt. Cover one side of the felt with fabric glue, and glue the felt piece on the puppet as shown in the diagram.

Attach pattern piece 6 B to the brown felt, and cut out the felt. Remove the pattern piece from the felt. Cover one side of the felt with fabric glue, and glue the felt piece on the puppet as shown in the diagram.

Attach pattern piece 18 I to the yellow felt, and cut out the felt. Remove the pattern piece from the felt. Cover one side of the felt with fabric glue, and glue the felt piece on the puppet as shown in the diagram.

Attach the diamond shape from the pattern pieces labeled 18 M to the red felt, and cut out the felt. Attach the circle shapes from the pattern pieces labeled 18 M to the purple felt, and cut out the felt. Remove the pattern pieces from the felt. Cover one side of the felt with fabric glue, and glue the felt pieces on the puppet as shown in the diagram. Add facial features using three-dimensional fabric paint, permanent markers, or felt scraps.

Pharaoh

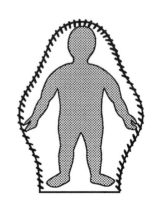

Materials:

- 2 light blue felt squares for puppet background

- Tan colored felt square for body and face

- Medium blue felt square for tunic and sash

- Yellow felt square for robe, collar, sash, and kilt

- Black felt for beard

- Light blue embroidery thread

- Scissors

- Straight pins or masking tape

- Large tapestry needle, size 18 or 20

- Fabric glue

- Puppet Background A on page 133. Pattern pieces 1 A and 1 C on page 136. Pattern pieces 15 C through 15 I on page 150. Pattern pieces 19 A, 19 B, 19 C, 19 D, 19 E, 19 F, 19 K, 19 L, 19 O, and 19 P on page 154.

Directions:

Sew the puppet background according to the directions on page 9. Photocopy or trace the Pharaoh pattern pieces, and cut them out. Pin or tape the pattern pieces to the felt, and then cut out the felt. Rolled pieces of masking tape can be attached at several points to the back of each pattern piece. This will enable the pattern piece to stick to the felt while cutting. Follow the directions beside each diagram for cutting and gluing the pattern pieces. You may want to cut out all the felt pieces, and practice placing them on the puppet before gluing each piece in place.

Attach pattern pieces 1 A and 1 C to the tan felt, and cut out the felt. Remove pattern piece 1 A from the tan felt. Cover one side of the felt with fabric glue, and glue the felt piece on the puppet as shown in the diagram. Save pattern piece 1 C for later.

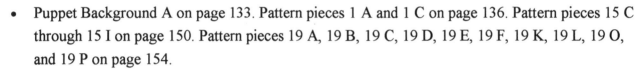

Easy-to-Make Bible Story Puppets

Attach pattern piece 19 A to the yellow felt, and cut out the felt. Remove the pattern piece from the felt. Cover one side of the felt with fabric glue, and glue the felt piece on the puppet as shown in the diagram.

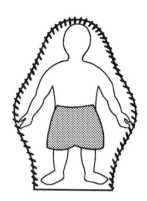

Attach pattern piece 19 F to the medium blue felt, and cut out the felt. Remove the pattern piece from the felt. Cover one side of the felt with fabric glue, and glue the felt piece on the puppet as shown in the diagram.

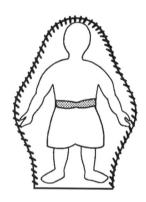

Attach pattern piece 19 C to the yellow felt, and cut out the felt. Remove the pattern piece from the felt. Cover one side of the felt with fabric glue, and glue the felt piece on the puppet as shown in the diagram.

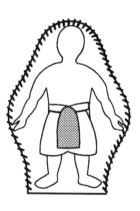

Attach pattern piece 19 D to the medium blue felt, and cut out the felt. Remove the pattern piece from the felt. Cover one side of the felt with fabric glue, and glue the felt piece on the puppet as shown in the diagram.

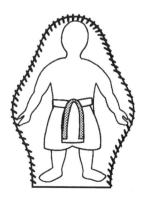

Attach pattern pieces 15 D and 15 G to the yellow felt, and cut out the felt. Remove the pattern pieces from the felt. Cover one side of the felt with fabric glue, and glue the felt pieces on the puppet as shown in the diagram.

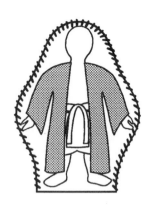

Attach pattern pieces 15 E and 15 F to the medium blue felt, and cut out the felt. Remove the pattern pieces from the felt. Cover one side of the felt with fabric glue, and glue the felt pieces on the puppet as shown in the diagram.

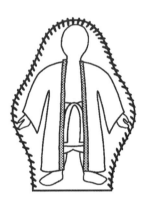

Attach pattern piece 19 B to the yellow felt, and cut out the felt. Remove the pattern piece from the felt. Cover one side of the felt with fabric glue, and glue the felt piece on the puppet as shown in the diagram.

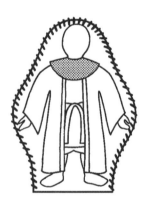

Attach pattern pieces 19 E, 15 C, and 15 H to the medium blue felt, and cut out the felt. Remove the pattern pieces from the felt. Cover one side of the felt with fabric glue, and glue the felt pieces on the puppet as shown in the diagram.

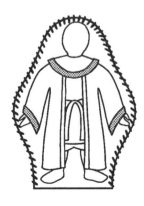

Easy-to-Make Bible Story Puppets

Remove pattern piece 1 C from the tan felt. Cover one side of the felt with fabric glue, and glue the felt piece on the puppet as shown in the diagram.

Attach pattern piece 19 L to the medium blue felt, and cut out the felt. Remove the pattern piece from the felt. Cover one side of the felt with fabric glue, and glue the felt piece on the puppet as shown in the diagram.

Attach pattern piece 19 O to the black felt, and cut out the felt. Attach pattern pieces 15 I and 19 K to the yellow felt, and cut out the felt. Remove the pattern pieces from the felt. Cover one side of the felt with fabric glue, and glue the felt pieces on the puppet as shown in the diagram.

Attach pattern piece 19 P to the yellow felt, and cut out the felt. Remove the pattern piece from the felt. Cover one side of the felt with fabric glue, and glue the felt piece on the puppet as shown in the diagram. Add sandal straps, stripes on headdress, and facial features using three-dimensional fabric paint, permanent markers, yarn, or felt scraps.

Priest

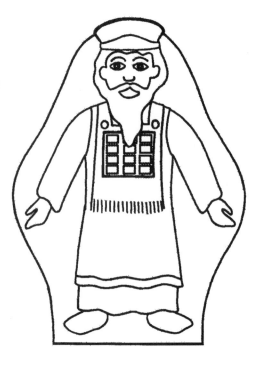

Possible Characters: Eli, Aaron, Zachariah, or any priest in the Old or New Testament.

Materials:

- 2 light blue felt squares for puppet background

- Peach colored felt square for body and face

- White felt square for robe and head covering

- Medium blue felt square for tunic and head covering

- Yellow felt for ephod

- Green, yellow, red, purple, blue, pink, orange, light green, maroon, light blue, turquoise, and lavender felt scraps for jewels on ephod

- Gray felt scraps for hair and beard

- Black felt scraps for shoes

- Light blue embroidery thread

- Scissors

- Straight pins or masking tape

- Large tapestry needle, size 18 or 20

- Fabric glue

Puppet Background A on page 133. Pattern pieces 1 A, 1 C, 1 D, and 1 E on page 136. Pattern piece 6 A on page 141. Pattern pieces 14 A, 14 B, 14 C, and 14 D on page 149. Pattern piece 16 B on page 151. Pattern pieces 17 B, 17 C, 17 D and 17 G on page 152.

Directions:

Sew the puppet background according to the directions on page 9. Photocopy or trace the Priest pattern pieces, and cut them out. Pin or tape the pattern pieces to the felt, and then cut out the felt. Rolled pieces of masking tape can be attached at several points to the back of each pattern piece. This will enable the pattern piece to stick to the felt while cutting. Follow the directions beside each diagram for cutting and gluing the pattern pieces. You may want to cut out all the felt pieces, and practice placing them on the puppet before gluing each piece in place.

Attach pattern pieces 1 A and 1 C to the peach felt, and cut out the felt. Remove pattern piece 1 A from the peach felt. Cover one side of the felt with fabric glue, and glue the felt piece on the puppet as shown in the diagram. Save pattern piece 1 C for the next step.

Easy-to-Make Bible Story Puppets

Remove pattern piece 1 C from the peach felt. Cover one side of the felt with fabric glue, and glue the felt piece on the puppet as shown in the diagram.

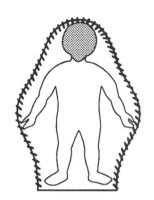

Attach pattern pieces 1 D and 1 E to the black felt, and cut out the felt. Remove the pattern pieces from the felt. Cover one side of the felt with fabric glue, and glue the felt pieces on the puppet as shown in the diagram.

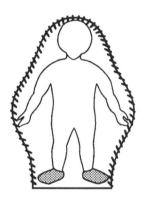

Attach pattern piece 16 B to the white felt, and cut out the felt. Remove the pattern piece from the felt. Cover one side of the felt with fabric glue, and glue the felt piece on the puppet as shown in the diagram.

Attach pattern piece 14 A to the medium blue felt, and cut out the felt. Remove the pattern piece from the felt. Cover one side of the felt with fabric glue, and glue the felt piece on the puppet as shown in the diagram.

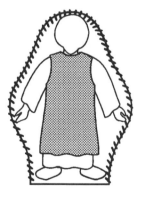

Attach pattern piece 17 C to the yellow felt, and cut out the felt. Remove the pattern piece from the felt. Cut fringe on the bottom of the ephod as shown on the pattern. Cover one side of the felt with fabric glue, and glue the felt piece on the puppet as shown in the diagram.

Attach pattern piece 17 B to the white felt, and cut out the felt. Attach pattern pieces labeled 17 D to the blue felt, and cut out the felt. Remove the pattern pieces from the felt. Cover one side of the felt with fabric glue, and glue the felt pieces on the puppet as shown in the diagram.

Attach pattern piece 14 B to the yellow felt, and cut out the felt. Remove the pattern piece from the felt. Cover one side of the felt with fabric glue, and glue the felt piece on the puppet as shown in the diagram.

Attach pattern piece 6 A to the gray felt, and cut out the felt. Remove the pattern piece from the felt. Cover one side of the felt with fabric glue, leaving the bottom of the beard free, and glue the felt piece on the puppet as shown in the diagram.

Attach pattern piece 14 C to the white felt, and cut out the felt. Remove the pattern piece from the felt. Cover one side of the felt with fabric glue, and glue the felt piece on the puppet as shown in the diagram.

Attach pattern piece 14 D to the medium blue felt, and cut out the felt. Remove the pattern piece from the felt. Cover one side of the felt with fabric glue, and glue the felt piece on the puppet as shown in the diagram. Use pattern piece 17 G to cut jewels for ephod out of 12 different colors of felt. Cover one side of each felt piece with fabric glue, and glue the felt pieces on the puppet as shown in the diagram. Add facial features using three-dimensional fabric paint, permanent markers, or felt scraps.

Easy-to-Make Bible Story Puppets

Messiah with Cross

Materials:

- 2 light blue felt squares for puppet background

- Peach colored felt square for body and face

- Tan felt square for cross

- Dark brown felt scraps for hair and beard

- Light brown felt for garment

- Green felt for crown of thorns

- Light blue embroidery thread

- Scissors

- Straight pins or masking tape

- Large tapestry needle, size 18 or 20

- Fabric glue

- Puppet Background A on page 133. Pattern pieces 1 A, and 1 C on page 136. Pattern pieces 6 A and 6 K on page 141. Pattern pieces 20 B and 20 C on page 155.

Directions:

Sew the puppet background according to the directions on page 9. Photocopy or trace the Messiah with Cross pattern pieces, and cut them out. Pin or tape the pattern pieces to the felt, and then cut out the felt. Rolled pieces of masking tape can be attached at several points to the back of each pattern piece. This will enable the pattern piece to stick to the felt while cutting. Follow the directions beside each diagram for cutting and gluing the pattern pieces. You may want to cut out all the felt pieces, and practice placing them on the puppet before gluing each piece in place.

Attach pattern piece 20 B to the tan felt, and cut out the felt. Remove the pattern piece from the felt. Cover one side of the felt with fabric glue, and glue the felt piece on the puppet as shown in the diagram. Part of the cross will overhang the puppet background, so do not put glue on this part.

Attach pattern pieces 1 A and 1 C to the peach felt, and cut out the felt. Remove pattern piece 1 A from the peach felt. Cover one side of the felt with fabric glue, and glue the felt piece on the puppet as shown in the diagram. Save pattern piece 1 C for the next step.

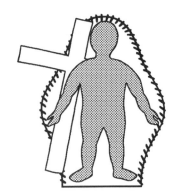

Remove pattern piece 1 C from the peach felt. Cover one side of the felt with fabric glue, and glue the felt piece on the puppet as shown in the diagram.

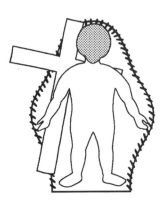

Attach pattern piece 6 A to the dark brown felt, and cut out the felt. Remove the pattern piece from the felt. Cover one side of the felt with fabric glue, and glue the felt piece on the puppet as shown in the diagram.

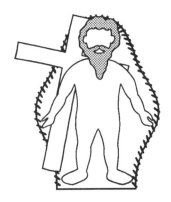

Attach pattern piece 6 K to the light brown felt, and cut out the felt. Remove the pattern piece from the felt. Cover one side of the felt with fabric glue, and glue the felt piece on the puppet as shown in the diagram.

Easy-to-Make Bible Story Puppets

Attach pattern piece 20 C to the green felt, and cut out the felt. Remove the pattern piece from the felt. Cover one side of the felt with fabric glue, and glue the felt piece on the puppet as shown in the diagram.

Add facial features using three-dimensional fabric paint, permanent markers, or felt scraps.

Burning Bush

Materials:

- 2 light blue felt squares for puppet background
- Yellow felt square for fire
- Orange felt square for fire
- Brown felt square for bush
- Light blue embroidery thread
- Scissors
- Straight pins or masking tape
- Large tapestry needle, size 18 or 20
- Fabric glue
- Puppet Background B on page 134. Pattern piece 27 A on page 162. Pattern piece 28 A and 28 B on page 163.

Directions:

Sew the puppet background according to the directions on page 9. Photocopy or trace the Burning Bush pattern pieces, and cut them out. Pin or tape the pattern pieces to the felt, and then cut out the felt. Rolled pieces of masking tape can be attached at several points to the back of each pattern piece. This will enable the pattern piece to stick to the felt while cutting. Follow the directions beside each diagram for cutting and gluing the pattern pieces. You may want to cut out all the felt pieces, and practice placing them on the puppet before gluing each piece in place.

Attach pattern piece 28 A to the yellow felt, and cut out the felt. Remove the pattern piece from the felt. Cover one side of the felt with fabric glue, and glue the felt piece on the puppet as shown in the diagram.

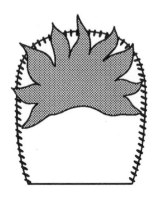

Attach pattern piece 28 B to the orange felt, and cut out the felt. Remove the pattern piece from the felt. Cover one side of the felt with fabric glue, and glue the felt piece on the puppet as shown in the diagram.

Attach pattern piece 27 A to the brown felt, and cut out the felt. Remove the pattern piece from the felt. Cover one side of the felt with fabric glue, and glue the felt piece on the puppet as shown in the diagram.

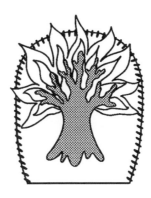

Camel

Materials:

- 2 light blue felt squares for puppet background
- Tan felt square for sand and camel nose
- Orange felt scraps for blanket
- 2 camel brown felt squares for camel
- Light blue embroidery thread
- Scissors
- Straight pins or masking tape
- Large tapestry needle, size 18 or 20
- Fabric glue
- Puppet Background B on page 134. Pattern pieces 36 A and 36 B on page 171. Pattern pieces 37 A, 37 B, and 37 C on page 172.

Directions:

Sew the puppet background according to the directions on page 9. Photocopy or trace the Camel pattern pieces, and cut them out. Pin or tape the pattern pieces to the felt, and then cut out the felt. Rolled pieces of masking tape can be attached at several points to the back of each pattern piece. This will enable the pattern piece to stick to the felt while cutting. Follow the directions beside each diagram for cutting and gluing the pattern pieces. You may want to cut out all the felt pieces, and practice placing them on the puppet before gluing each piece in place.

Attach pattern piece 36 B to the tan felt, and cut out the felt. Remove the pattern piece from the felt. Cover one side of the felt with fabric glue, and glue the felt piece on the puppet as shown in the diagram.

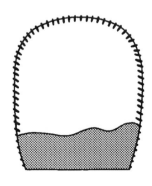

Easy-to-Make Bible Story Puppets

Attach pattern piece 36 A to the camel brown felt, and cut out the felt. Remove the pattern piece from the felt. Cover one side of the felt with fabric glue, and glue the felt piece on the puppet as shown in the diagram.

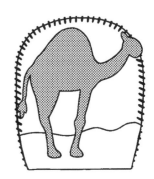

Attach pattern piece 37 A to the camel brown felt, and cut out the felt. Remove the pattern piece from the felt. Cover one side of the felt with fabric glue, and glue the felt piece on the puppet as shown in the diagram.

Attach pattern piece 37 C to the orange felt, and cut out the felt. Remove the pattern piece from the felt. Cover one side of the felt with fabric glue, and glue the felt piece on the puppet as shown in the diagram.

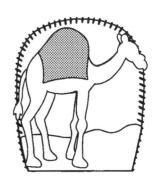

Attach pattern piece 37 B to the tan felt, and cut out the felt. Remove the pattern piece from the felt. Cover one side of the felt with fabric glue, and glue the felt piece on the puppet as shown in the diagram.

Add facial features using three-dimensional fabric paint, permanent markers, or felt scraps.

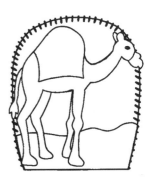

Cow

Materials:

- 2 light blue felt squares for puppet background
- 2 brown felt squares for cow
- Green felt square for grass
- Tan felt scraps for top knot
- Tan felt scraps for nose
- Black felt scraps for hooves
- White felt for horns
- Light blue embroidery thread
- Scissors
- Straight pins or masking tape
- Large tapestry needle, size 18 or 20
- Fabric glue
- Puppet Background B on page 134. Pattern pieces 38 A through 38 E on page 173. Pattern pieces 39 A through 39 F on page 174.

Directions:

Sew the puppet background according to the directions on page 9. Photocopy or trace the Cow pattern pieces, and cut them out. Pin or tape the pattern pieces to the felt, and then cut out the felt. Rolled pieces of masking tape can be attached at several points to the back of each pattern piece. This will enable the pattern piece to stick to the felt while cutting. Follow the directions beside each diagram for cutting and gluing the pattern pieces. You may want to cut out all the felt pieces, and practice placing them on the puppet before gluing each piece in place.

Attach pattern piece 39 A to the brown felt, and cut out the felt. Remove the pattern piece from the felt. Cover one side of the felt with fabric glue, and glue the felt piece on the puppet as shown in the diagram.

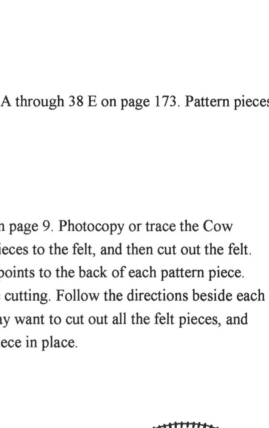

Easy-to-Make Bible Story Puppets

Attach pattern piece 38 A to the brown felt, and cut out the felt. Remove the pattern piece from the felt. Cover one side of the felt with fabric glue, and glue the felt piece on the puppet as shown in the diagram.

Attach pattern piece 38 E to the white felt, and cut out the felt. Remove the pattern piece from the felt. Cover one side of the felt with fabric glue, and glue the felt piece on the puppet as shown in the diagram.

Attach pattern piece 38 B to the brown felt, and cut out the felt. Remove the pattern piece from the felt. Cover one side of the felt with fabric glue, and glue the felt piece on the puppet as shown in the diagram.

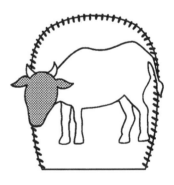

Attach pattern piece 38 D to the tan felt, and cut out the felt. Remove the pattern piece from the felt. Cover one side of the felt with fabric glue, and glue the felt piece on the puppet as shown in the diagram.

Attach pattern piece 38 C to the tan felt, and cut out the felt. Remove the pattern piece from the felt. Cover one side of the felt with fabric glue, and glue the felt piece on the puppet as shown in the diagram.

Attach pattern pieces 39 B, 39 C, 39 D, and 39 E to the black felt, and cut out the felt. Remove the pattern pieces from the felt. Cover one side of the felt with fabric glue, and glue the felt pieces on the puppet as shown in the diagram.

Attach pattern piece 39 F to the green felt, and cut out the felt. Remove the pattern piece from the felt. Cover one side of the felt with fabric glue, and glue the felt piece on the puppet as shown in the diagram.

Add facial features using three-dimensional fabric paint, permanent markers, or felt scraps.

Donkey

Materials:

- 2 light blue felt squares for puppet background
- 2 gray felt squares for donkey
- Green felt square for grass
- Black felt scraps for hooves, tail, and mane
- Light blue embroidery thread
- Scissors
- Straight pins or masking tape
- Large tapestry needle, size 18 or 20
- Fabric glue
- Puppet Background B on page 134. Pattern pieces 31 A and 31 C on page 166. Pattern pieces 32 A through 32 G on page 167. Pattern piece 39 F on page 174.

Directions:

Sew the puppet background according to the directions on page 9. Photocopy or trace the Donkey pattern pieces, and cut them out. Pin or tape the pattern pieces to the felt, and then cut out the felt. Rolled pieces of masking tape can be attached at several points to the back of each pattern piece. This will enable the pattern piece to stick to the felt while cutting. Follow the directions beside each diagram for cutting and gluing the pattern pieces. You may want to cut out all the felt pieces, and practice placing them on the puppet before gluing each piece in place.

Attach pattern piece 39 F to the green felt, and cut out the felt. Remove the pattern piece from the felt. Cover one side of the felt with fabric glue, and glue the felt piece on the puppet as shown in the diagram.

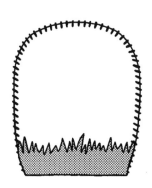

Attach pattern piece 31 A to the gray felt, and cut out the felt. Remove the pattern piece from the felt. Cover one side of the felt with fabric glue, and glue the felt piece on the puppet as shown in the diagram.

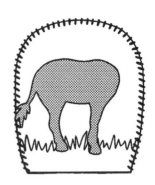

Attach pattern piece 32 A to the gray felt, and cut out the felt. Remove the pattern piece from the felt. Cover one side of the felt with fabric glue, and glue the felt piece on the puppet as shown in the diagram.

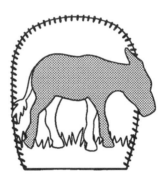

Attach pattern piece 32 B to the black felt, and cut out the felt. Remove the pattern piece from the felt. Cover one side of the felt with fabric glue, and glue the felt piece on the puppet as shown in the diagram.

Attach pattern piece 32 G to the gray felt, and cut out the felt. Remove the pattern piece from the felt. Cover one side of the felt with fabric glue, and glue the felt piece on the puppet as shown in the diagram.

Easy-to-Make Bible Story Puppets

Attach pattern piece 31 C to the black felt, and cut out the felt. Remove the pattern piece from the felt. Cover one side of the felt with fabric glue, and glue the felt piece on the puppet as shown in the diagram.

Attach pattern pieces 32 C, 32 D, 32 E, and 32 F to the black felt, and cut out the felt. Remove the pattern pieces from the felt. Cover one side of the felt with fabric glue, and glue the felt pieces on the puppet as shown in the diagram.

Add facial features using three-dimensional fabric paint, permanent markers, or felt scraps.

Dove

Materials:

- 2 light blue felt squares for puppet background
- White felt square for dove and clouds
- Green felt scrap for olive branch
- Yellow felt scraps for the beak and feet
- Light blue embroidery thread
- Scissors
- Straight pins or masking tape
- Large tapestry needle, size 18 or 20
- Fabric glue

Puppet Background A on page 133. Pattern pieces 35 A through 35 H on page 170.

Directions:

Sew the puppet background according to the directions on page 9. Photocopy or trace the Dove pattern pieces, and cut them out. Pin or tape the pattern pieces to the felt, and then cut out the felt. Rolled pieces of masking tape can be attached at several points to the back of each pattern piece. This will enable the pattern piece to stick to the felt while cutting. Follow the directions beside each diagram for cutting and gluing the pattern pieces. You may want to cut out all the felt pieces, and practice placing them on the puppet before gluing each piece in place.

Attach pattern pieces 35 A and 35 B to the white felt, and cut out the felt. Remove the pattern pieces from the felt. Cover one side of the felt with fabric glue, and glue the felt pieces on the puppet as shown in the diagram.

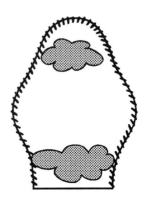

Attach pattern piece 35 D to the white felt, and cut out the felt. Remove the pattern piece from the felt. Cover one side of the felt with fabric glue, and glue the felt piece on the puppet as shown in the diagram.

Attach pattern piece 35 E to the white felt, and cut out the felt. Remove the pattern piece from the felt. Cover one side of the felt with fabric glue, and glue the felt piece on the puppet as shown in the diagram.

Attach pattern piece 35 C to the green felt, and cut out the felt. Remove the pattern piece from the felt. Cover one side of the felt with fabric glue, and glue the felt piece on the puppet as shown in the diagram.

Attach pattern piece 35 F, 35 G, and 35 H to the yellow felt, and cut out the felt. Remove the pattern pieces from the felt. Cover one side of the felt with fabric glue, and glue the felt pieces on the puppet as shown in the diagram. Add facial features using three-dimensional fabric paint, permanent markers, or felt scraps.

Lion

Materials:

- 2 light blue felt squares for puppet background
- Gray felt square for rock
- Tan felt square for lion
- Brown felt square for mane
- Peach felt scraps for tongue and nose
- Light blue embroidery thread
- Scissors
- Straight pins or masking tape
- Large tapestry needle, size 18 or 20
- Fabric glue

Puppet Background B on page 134. Pattern piece 26 A on page 161. Pattern pieces 29 A through 29 E on page 164.

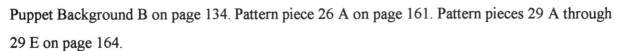

Directions:

Sew the puppet background according to the directions on page 9. Photocopy or trace the Lion pattern pieces, and cut them out. Pin or tape the pattern pieces to the felt, and then cut out the felt. Rolled pieces of masking tape can be attached at several points to the back of each pattern piece. This will enable the pattern piece to stick to the felt while cutting. Follow the directions beside each diagram for cutting and gluing the pattern pieces. You may want to cut out all the felt pieces, and practice placing them on the puppet before gluing each piece in place.

Attach pattern piece 26 A to the gray felt, and cut out the felt. Remove the pattern piece from the felt. Cover one side of the felt with fabric glue, and glue the felt piece on the puppet as shown in the diagram.

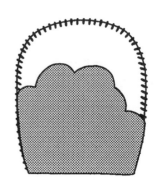

Easy-to-Make Bible Story Puppets

Attach pattern piece 29 A to the tan felt, and cut out the felt. Remove the pattern piece from the felt. Cover one side of the felt with fabric glue, and glue the felt piece on the puppet as shown in the diagram.

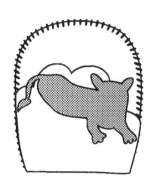

Attach pattern piece 29 B to the tan felt, and cut out the felt. Remove the pattern piece from the felt. Cover one side of the felt with fabric glue, and glue the felt piece on the puppet as shown in the diagram.

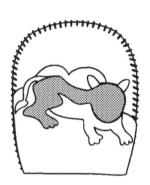

Attach pattern piece 29 C to the brown felt, and cut out the felt. Remove the pattern piece from the felt. Cover one side of the felt with fabric glue, and glue the felt piece on the puppet as shown in the diagram.

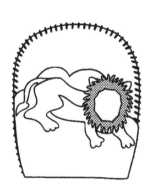

Attach pattern piece 29 E to the peach felt, and cut out the felt. Remove the pattern piece from the felt. Cover one side of the felt with fabric glue, and glue the felt piece on the puppet as shown in the diagram.

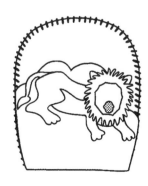

Attach pattern piece 29 D to the brown felt, and cut out the felt. Remove the pattern piece from the felt. Cover one side of the felt with fabric glue, and glue the felt piece on the puppet as shown in the diagram.

Add facial features using three-dimensional fabric paint, permanent marker, or felt scraps.

Easy-to-Make Bible Story Puppets

Loaves and Fishes

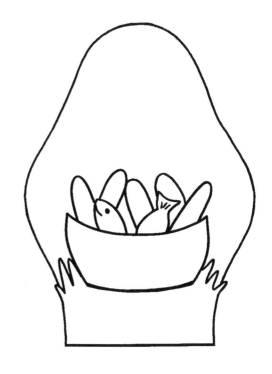

Materials:

- 2 light blue felt squares for puppet background
- Green felt square for grass
- Gray felt scraps for fish
- Brown felt square for basket
- Tan felt scraps for bread
- Light blue embroidery thread
- Scissors
- Straight pins or masking tape
- Large tapestry needle, size 18 or 20
- Fabric glue

Puppet Background A on page 133. Pattern pieces 30 D through 30 K on page 165. Pattern piece 31 B on page 166.

Directions:

Sew the puppet background according to the directions on page 9. Photocopy or trace the Loaves and Fishes pattern pieces, and cut them out. Pin or tape the pattern pieces to the felt, and then cut out the felt. Rolled pieces of masking tape can be attached at several points to the back of each pattern piece. This will enable the pattern piece to stick to the felt while cutting. Follow the directions beside each diagram for cutting and gluing the pattern pieces. You may want to cut out all the felt pieces, and practice placing them on the puppet before gluing each piece in place.

Attach pattern piece 31 B to the green felt, and cut out the felt. Remove the pattern piece from the felt. Cover one side of the felt with fabric glue, and glue the felt piece on the puppet as shown in the diagram.

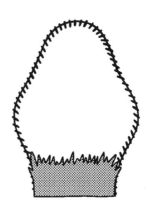

Attach pattern pieces 30 E, 30 F, 30 G, 30 I, and 30 J to the tan felt, and cut out the felt. Remove the pattern pieces from the felt. Cover one side of the felt with fabric glue, and glue the felt pieces on the puppet as shown in the diagram.

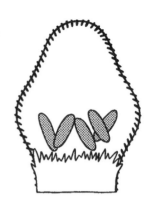

Attach pattern pieces 30 H and 30 K to the gray felt, and cut out the felt. Remove the pattern pieces from the felt. Cover one side of the felt with fabric glue, and glue the felt pieces on the puppet as shown in the diagram.

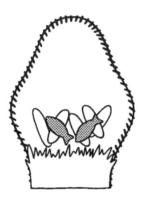

Attach pattern piece 30 D to the brown felt, and cut out the felt. Remove the pattern piece from the felt. Cover one side of the felt with fabric glue, and glue the felt piece on the puppet as shown in the diagram.

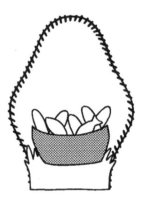

Add features on the fish face and fish tail using three-dimensional fabric paint, permanent markers, or felt scraps.

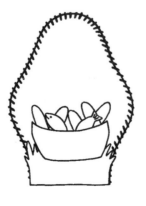

Easy-to-Make Bible Story Puppets

Pig

Materials:

- 2 light blue felt squares for puppet background
- Peach colored felt square for pig body and head
- Pink felt scraps for snout and ears
- Green felt square for grass
- Black felt scraps for feet
- Light blue embroidery thread
- Scissors
- Straight pins or masking tape
- Large tapestry needle, size 18 or 20
- Fabric glue

Puppet Background A on page 133. Pattern piece 31 B on page 166. Pattern piece 34 A through 34 I on page 169.

Directions:

Sew the puppet background according to the directions on page 9. Photocopy or trace the Pig pattern pieces, and cut them out. Pin or tape the pattern pieces to the felt, and then cut out the felt. Rolled pieces of masking tape can be attached at several points to the back of each pattern piece. This will enable the pattern piece to stick to the felt while cutting. Follow the directions beside each diagram for cutting and gluing the pattern pieces. You may want to cut out all the felt pieces, and practice placing them on the puppet before gluing each piece in place.

Attach pattern piece 34 E to the peach colored felt, and cut out the felt. Remove the pattern piece from the felt. Cover one side of the felt with fabric glue, and glue the felt piece on the puppet as shown in the diagram.

Attach pattern pieces 34 C and 34 D to the black felt, and cut out the felt. Remove the pattern pieces from the felt. Cover one side of the felt with fabric glue, and glue the felt pieces on the puppet as shown in the diagram.

Attach pattern piece 34 A to the peach colored felt, and cut out the felt. Remove the pattern piece from the felt. Cover one side of the felt with fabric glue, and glue the felt piece on the puppet as shown in the diagram.

Attach pattern piece 34 B to the pink felt, and cut out the felt. Remove the pattern piece from the felt. Cover one side of the felt with fabric glue, and glue the felt piece on the puppet as shown in the diagram.

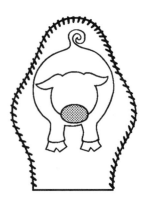

Attach pattern piece 31 B to the green felt, and cut out the felt. Remove the pattern piece from the felt. Cover one side of the felt with fabric glue, and glue the felt piece on the puppet as shown in the diagram.

Easy-to-Make Bible Story Puppets

Attach pattern pieces 34 F and 34 G to the black felt, and cut out the felt. Remove the pattern pieces from the felt. Cover one side of the felt with fabric glue, and glue the felt pieces on the puppet as shown in the diagram.

 Attach pattern pieces 34 H and 34 I to the pink felt, and cut out the felt. Remove the pattern pieces from the felt. Cover one side of the felt with fabric glue, and glue the felt pieces on the puppet as shown in the diagram. Add facial features using three-dimensional fabric paint, permanent markers, or felt scraps.

Serpent in Tree

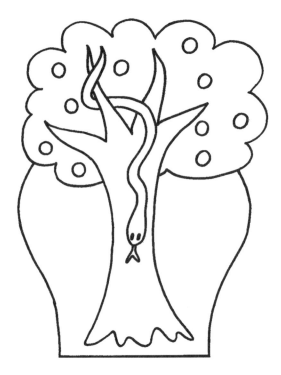

Materials:

- 2 light blue felt squares for puppet background
- Brown felt square tree trunk
- Green felt square for tree top
- Red felt scraps for fruit and serpent tongue
- Light green felt square for serpent
- Light blue embroidery thread
- Scissors
- Straight pins or masking tape
- Large tapestry needle, size 18 or 20
- Fabric glue

Puppet Background A on page 133. Pattern pieces 24 A through 24 D on page 159. Pattern piece 25 A on page 160.

Directions:

Sew the puppet background according to the directions on page 9. Photocopy or trace the Serpent in Tree pattern pieces, and cut them out. Pin or tape the pattern pieces to the felt, and then cut out the felt. Rolled pieces of masking tape can be attached at several points to the back of each pattern piece. This will enable the pattern piece to stick to the felt while cutting. Follow the directions beside each diagram for cutting and gluing the pattern pieces. You may want to cut out all the felt pieces, and practice placing them on the puppet before gluing each piece in place.

Attach pattern piece 25 A to the green felt, and cut out the felt. Remove the pattern piece from the felt. Cover one side of the felt with fabric glue, and glue the felt piece on the puppet as shown in the diagram. Part of the felt will overhang the puppet background, so do not put glue on this part.

Easy-to-Make Bible Story Puppets

Attach pattern piece 24 A to the brown felt, and cut out the felt. Remove the pattern piece from the felt. Cover one side of the felt with fabric glue, and glue the felt piece on the puppet as shown in the diagram.

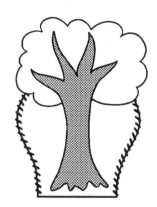

Attach pattern pieces labeled 24 B to the red felt, and cut out the felt. Remove the pattern pieces from the felt. Cover one side of the felt with fabric glue, and glue the felt pieces on the puppet as shown in the diagram.

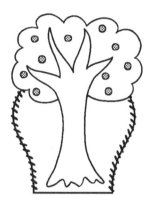

Attach pattern piece 24 C to the light green felt, and cut out the felt. Remove the pattern piece from the felt. Cover one side of the felt with fabric glue, and glue the felt piece on the puppet as shown in the diagram.

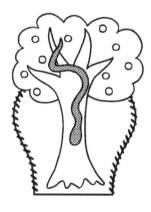

Attach pattern piece 24 D to the red felt, and cut out the felt. Remove the pattern piece from the felt. Cover one side of the felt with fabric glue, and glue the felt piece on the puppet as shown in the diagram. Add eyes on the serpent using three-dimensional fabric paint, permanent markers, or felt scraps.

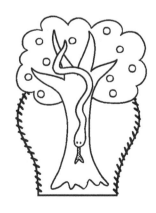

Sheep

Materials:

- 2 light blue felt squares for puppet background
- Green felt square for grass
- White felt square for sheep and eyes
- Black felt scraps for head and legs
- Light blue embroidery thread
- Scissors
- Straight pins or masking tape
- Large tapestry needle, size 18 or 20
- Fabric glue

Puppet Background A on page 133. Pattern pieces 30 A, 30 B, and 30 C on page 165. Pattern piece 31 B on page 166.

Directions:

Sew the puppet background according to the directions on page 9. Photocopy or trace the Sheep pattern pieces, and cut them out. Pin or tape the pattern pieces to the felt, and then cut out the felt. Rolled pieces of masking tape can be attached at several points to the back of each pattern piece. This will enable the pattern piece to stick to the felt while cutting. Follow the directions beside each diagram for cutting and gluing the pattern pieces. You may want to cut out all the felt pieces, and practice placing them on the puppet before gluing each piece in place.

Attach pattern piece 30 C to the black felt, and cut out the felt. Remove the pattern piece from the felt. Cover one side of the felt with fabric glue, and glue the felt piece on the puppet as shown in the diagram.

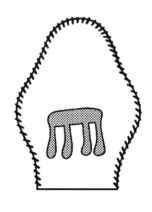

Easy-to-Make Bible Story Puppets

Attach pattern piece 31 B to the green felt, and cut out the felt. Remove the pattern piece from the felt. Cover one side of the felt with fabric glue, and glue the felt piece on the puppet as shown in the diagram.

Attach pattern piece 30 A to the white felt, and cut out the felt. Remove the pattern piece from the felt. Cover one side of the felt with fabric glue, and glue the felt piece on the puppet as shown in the diagram.

Attach pattern piece 30 B to the black felt, and cut out the felt. Remove the pattern piece from the felt. Cover one side of the felt with fabric glue, and glue the felt piece on the puppet as shown in the diagram.

Add facial features using white felt scraps.

Whale

Materials:

- 2 light blue felt squares for puppet background
- Gray felt square for whale
- White felt scraps for water spout and eye
- Black felt scrap for eye
- Light blue embroidery thread
- Scissors
- Straight pins or masking tape
- Large tapestry needle, size 18 or 20
- Fabric glue

Puppet Background B on page 134. Pattern pieces 33 A through 33 E on page 168.

Directions:

Sew the puppet background according to the directions on page 9. Photocopy or trace the Whale pattern pieces, and cut them out. Pin or tape the pattern pieces to the felt, and then cut out the felt. Rolled pieces of masking tape can be attached at several points to the back of each pattern piece. This will enable the pattern piece to stick to the felt while cutting. Follow the directions beside each diagram for cutting and gluing the pattern pieces. You may want to cut out all the felt pieces, and practice placing them on the puppet before gluing each piece in place.

Attach pattern piece 33 A to the gray felt, and cut out the felt. Remove the pattern piece from the felt. Cover one side of the felt with fabric glue, omitting glue on the tail, and glue the felt piece on the puppet as shown in the diagram. A portion of the felt will overhang the puppet background.

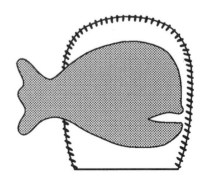

Easy-to-Make Bible Story Puppets

Attach pattern piece 33 C to the white felt, and cut out the felt. Remove the pattern piece from the felt. Cover one side of the felt with fabric glue, and glue the felt piece on the puppet as shown in the diagram.

Attach pattern piece 33 B to the gray felt, and cut out the felt. Remove the pattern piece from the felt. Cover one side of the felt with fabric glue, and glue the felt piece on the puppet as shown in the diagram.

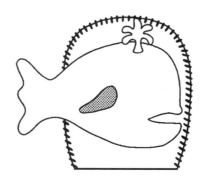

Attach pattern piece 33 E to the white felt, and cut out the felt. Remove the pattern piece from the felt. Cover one side of the felt with fabric glue, and glue the felt piece on the puppet as shown in the diagram.

Attach pattern piece 33 D to the black felt, and cut out the felt. Remove the pattern piece from the felt. Cover one side of the felt with fabric glue, and glue the felt piece on the puppet as shown in the diagram.

Bible Story Puppet Patterns

The puppet patterns on the following pages may be photocopied for use by a family or for a single classroom use. Once you have copied the patterns and cut them out, place the patterns from each page in an envelope and label the envelope (for example: 16 A, 16 B). This will enable you to easily find the pattern pieces you need, and store them for future use.

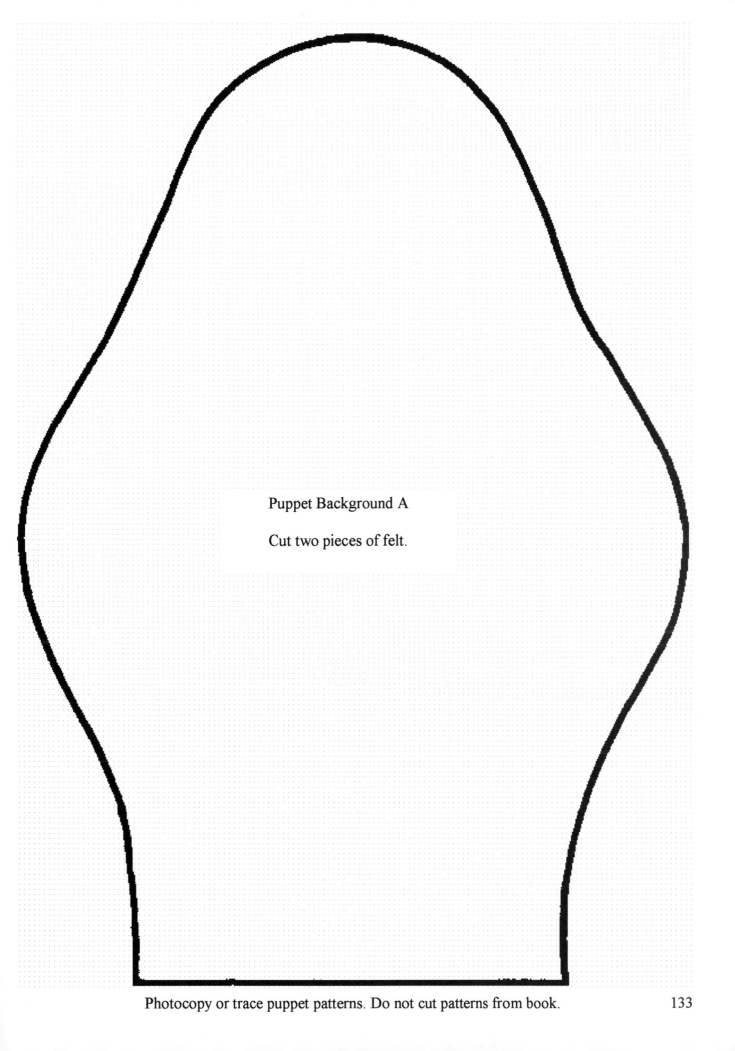

Puppet Background A

Cut two pieces of felt.

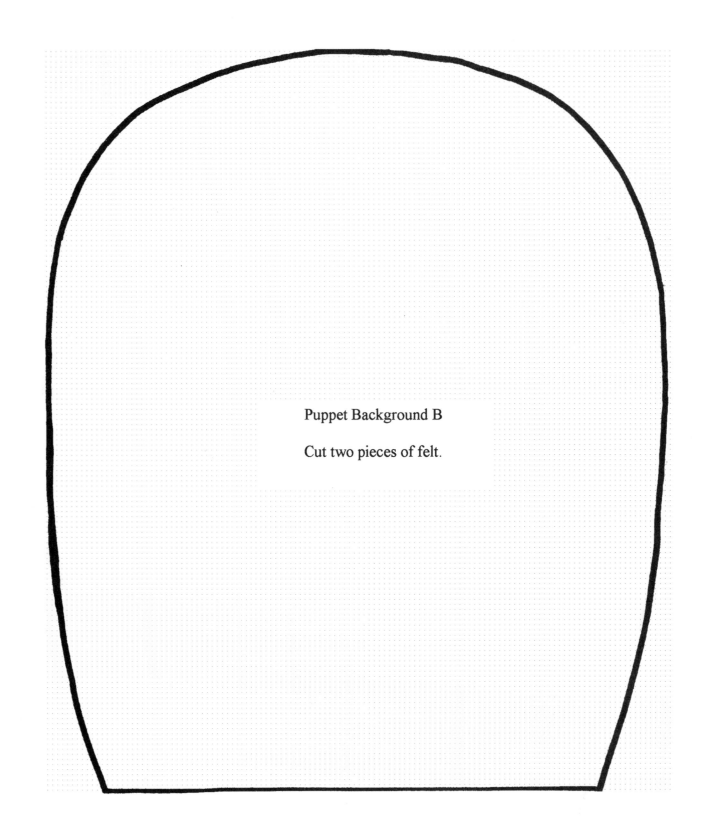

Puppet Background B

Cut two pieces of felt.

Photocopy or trace puppet patterns. Do not cut patterns from book.

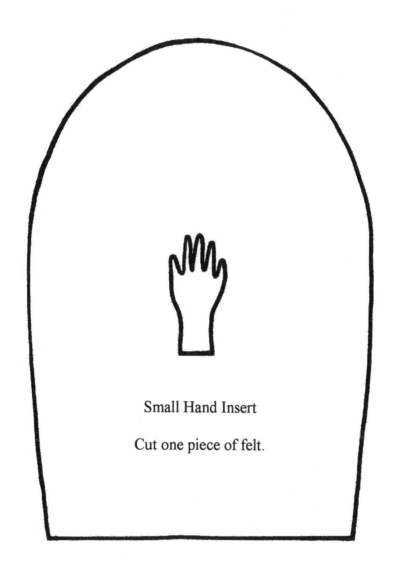

Small Hand Insert

Cut one piece of felt.

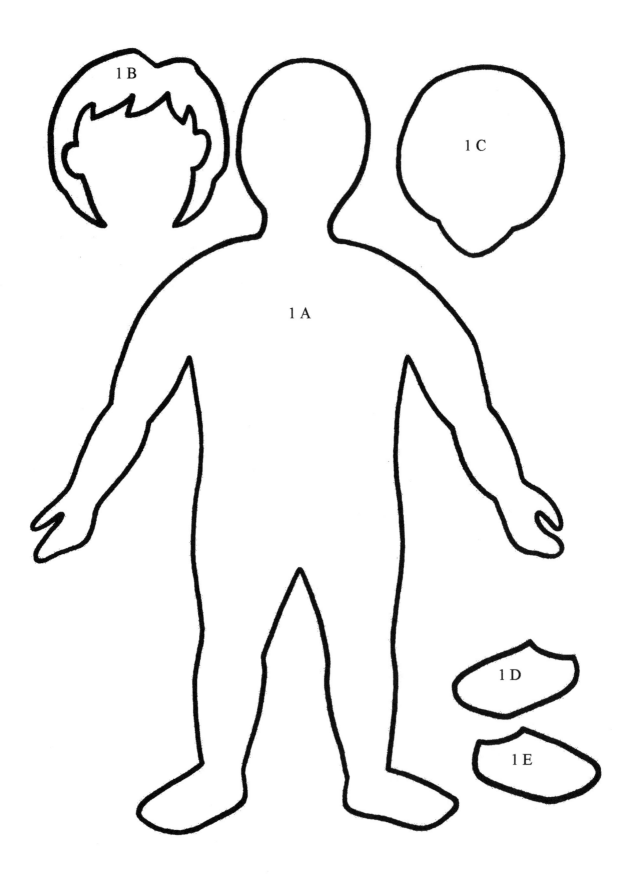

1 B

1 C

1 A

1 D

1 E

Photocopy or trace puppet patterns. Do not cut patterns from book.

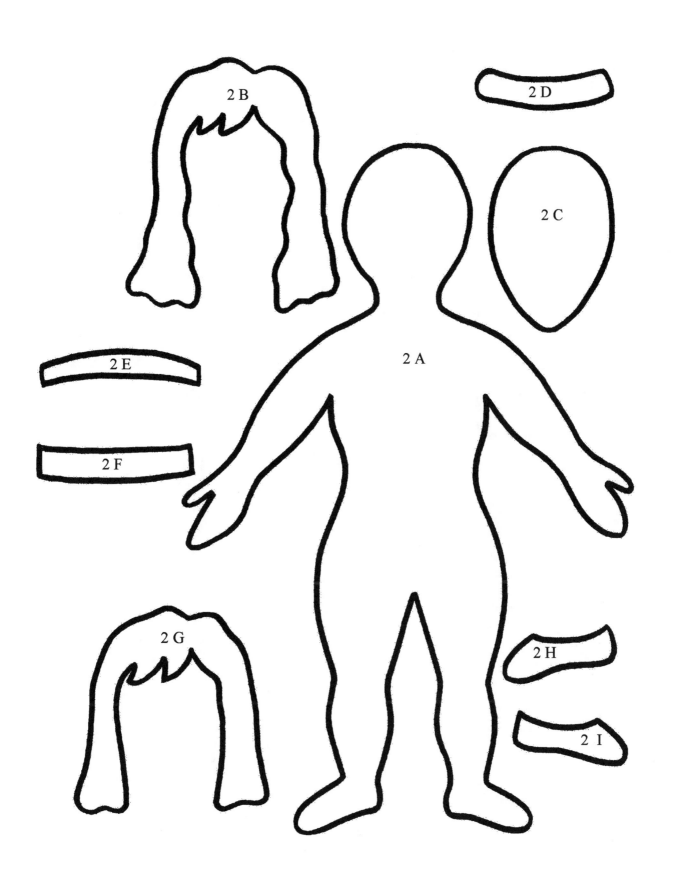

2 B

2 D

2 C

2 A

2 E

2 F

2 G

2 H

2 I

Photocopy or trace puppet patterns. Do not cut patterns from book.   137

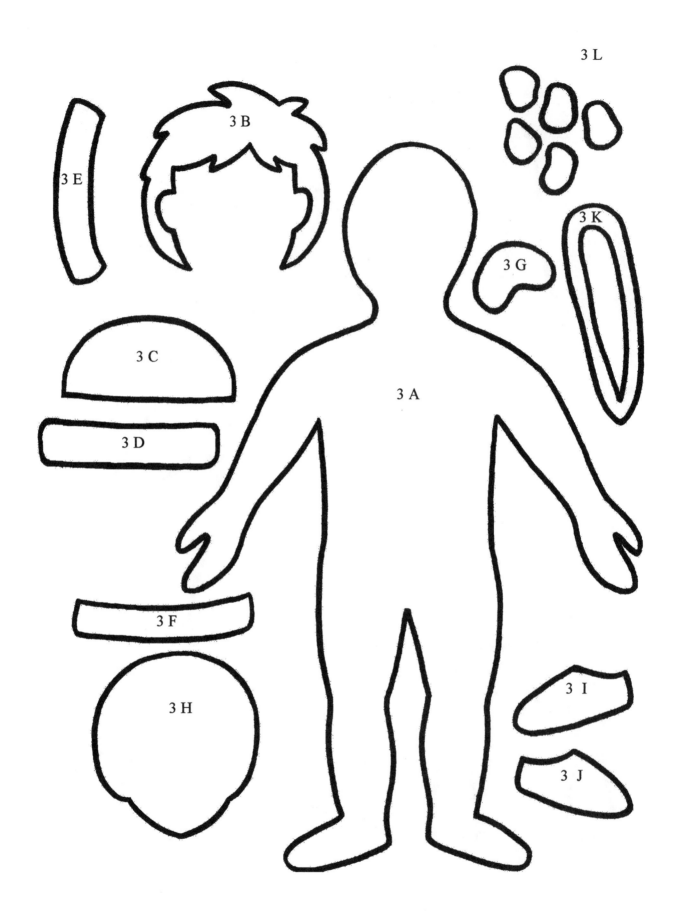

3 L

3 B

3 E

3 K

3 G

3 C

3 A

3 D

3 F

3 H

3 I

3 J

Photocopy or trace puppet patterns. Do not cut patterns from book.

4 C

4 B

4 D

4 A

4 E

4 F

4 G

4 H

Photocopy or trace puppet patterns. Do not cut patterns from book.

Photocopy or trace puppet patterns. Do not cut patterns from book.

6 A

6 B

6 C

6 D

6 E

6 F

6 G

6 H

6 I

6 J

6 K

6 L

Photocopy or trace puppet patterns. Do not cut patterns from book.

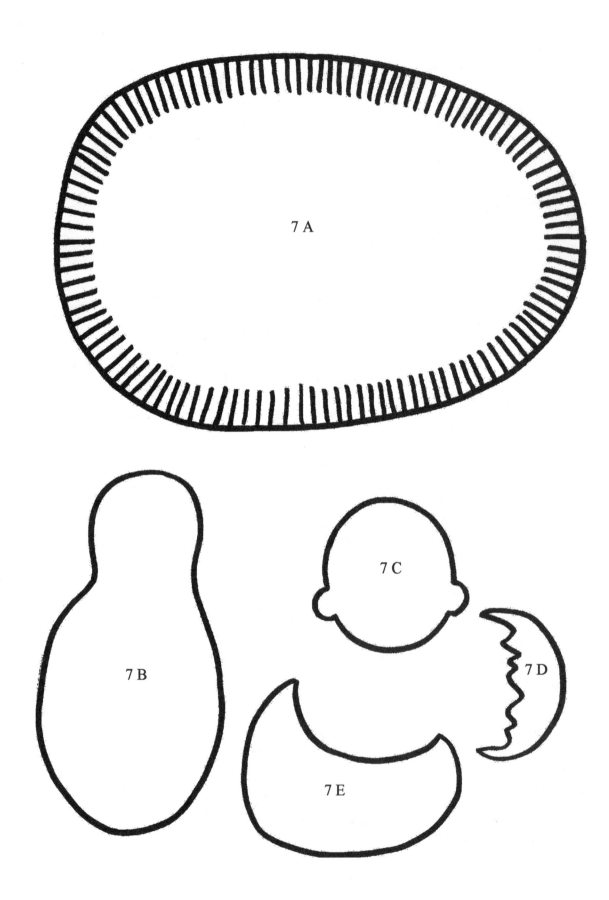

7 A

7 B

7 C

7 D

7 E

Photocopy or trace puppet patterns. Do not cut patterns from book.

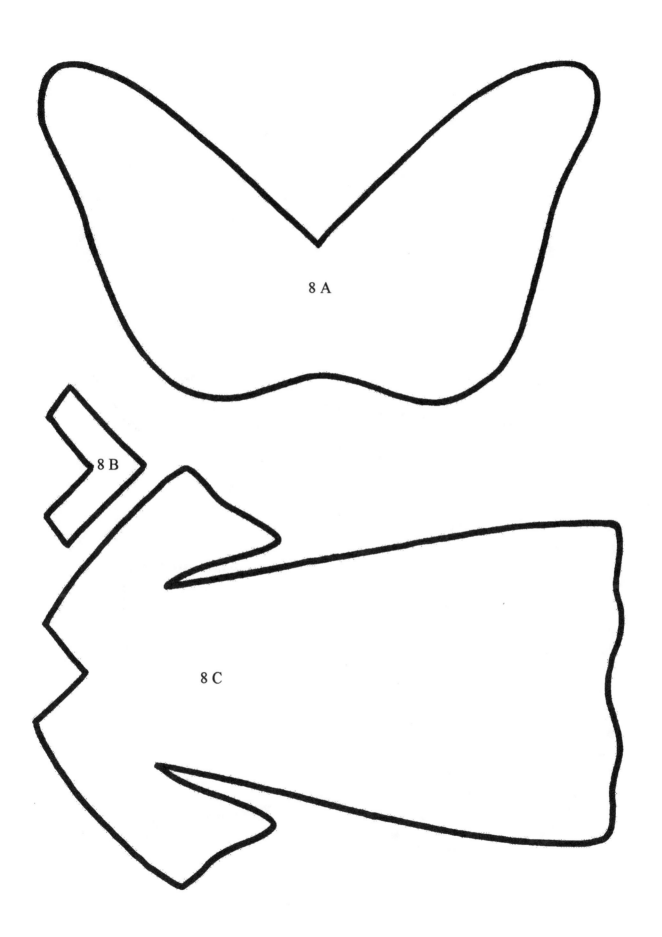

8 A

8 B

8 C

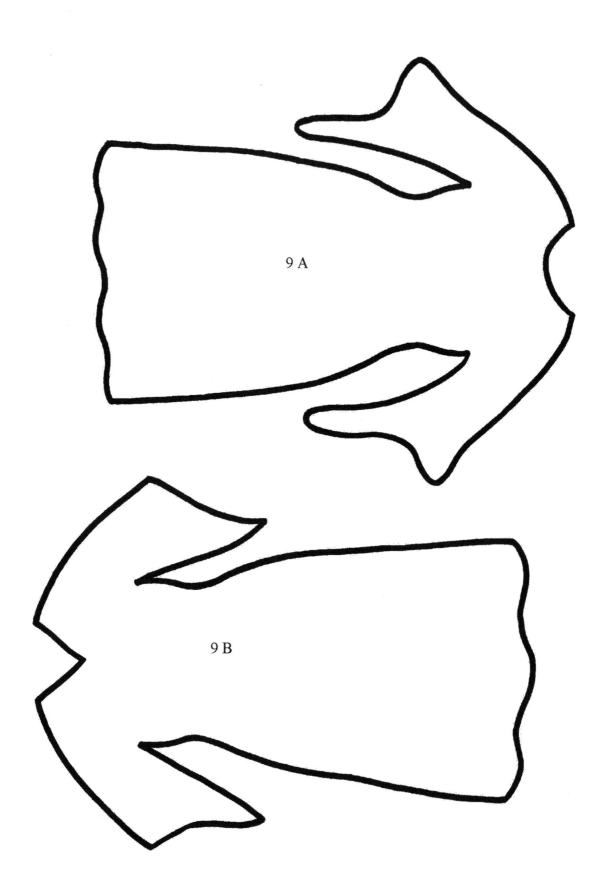

9 A

9 B

Photocopy or trace puppet patterns. Do not cut patterns from book.

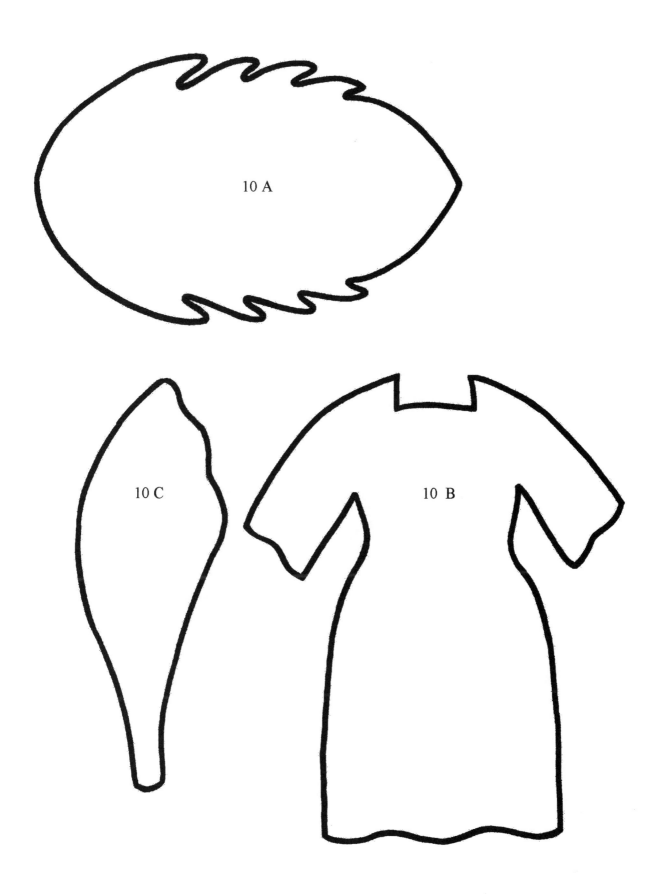

10 A

10 C

10 B

Photocopy or trace puppet patterns. Do not cut patterns from book.

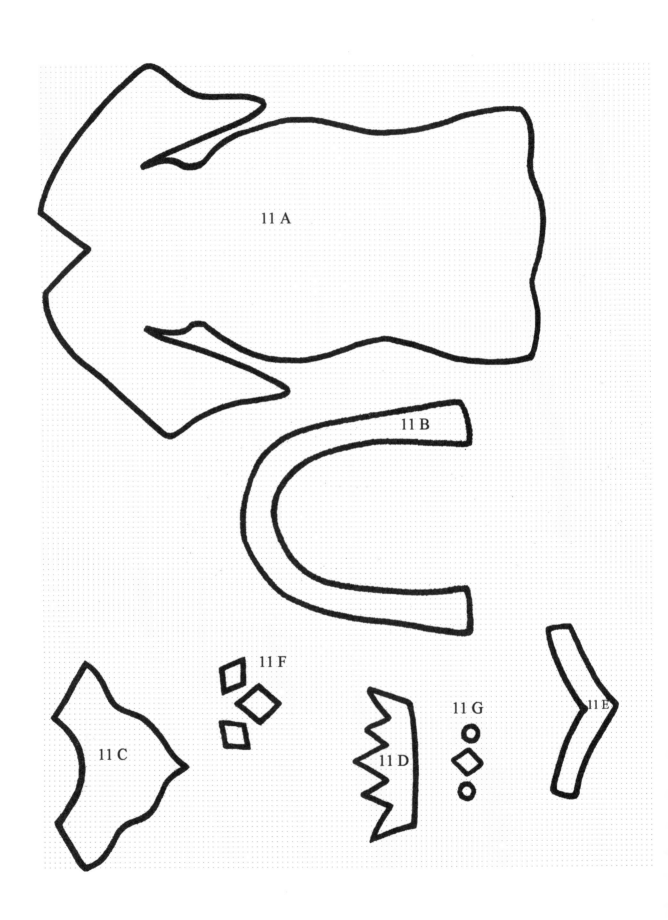

11 A

11 B

11 C

11 F

11 D

11 G

11 E

Photocopy or trace puppet patterns. Do not cut patterns from book.

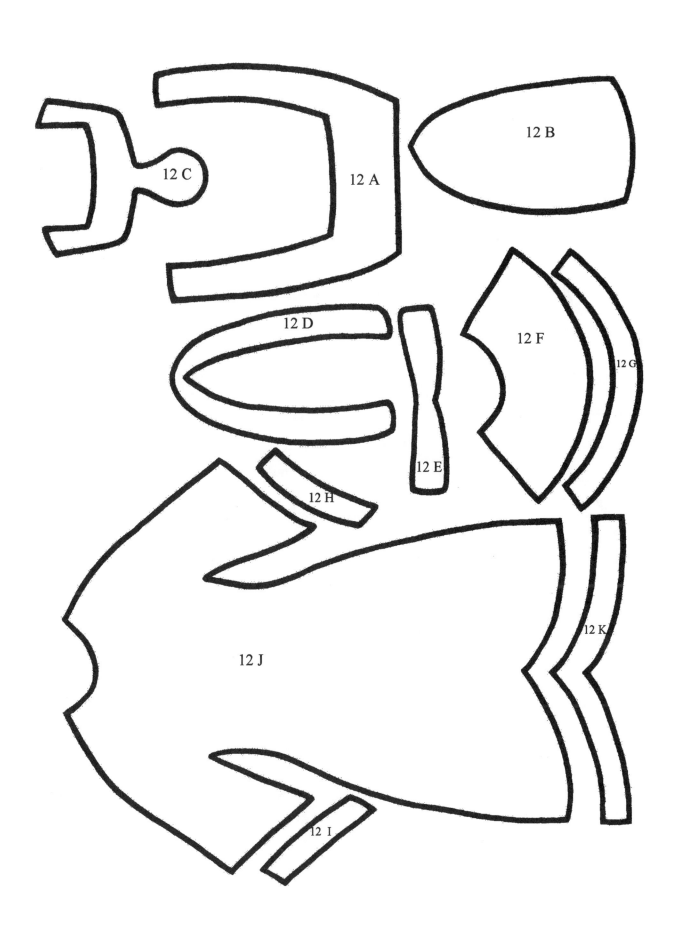

12 C

12 A

12 B

12 D

12 E

12 F

12 G

12 H

12 J

12 K

12 I

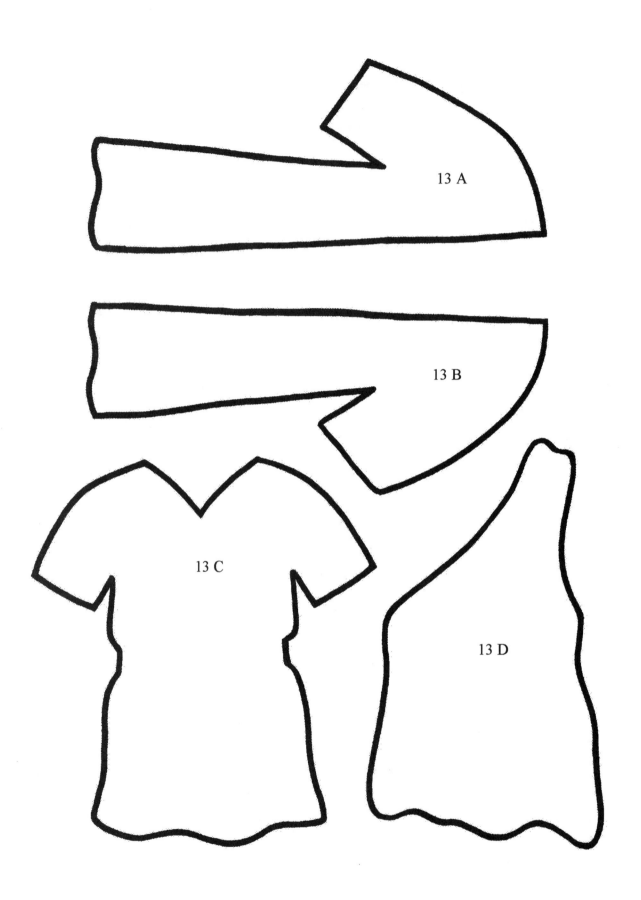

13 A

13 B

13 C

13 D

Photocopy or trace puppet patterns. Do not cut patterns from book.

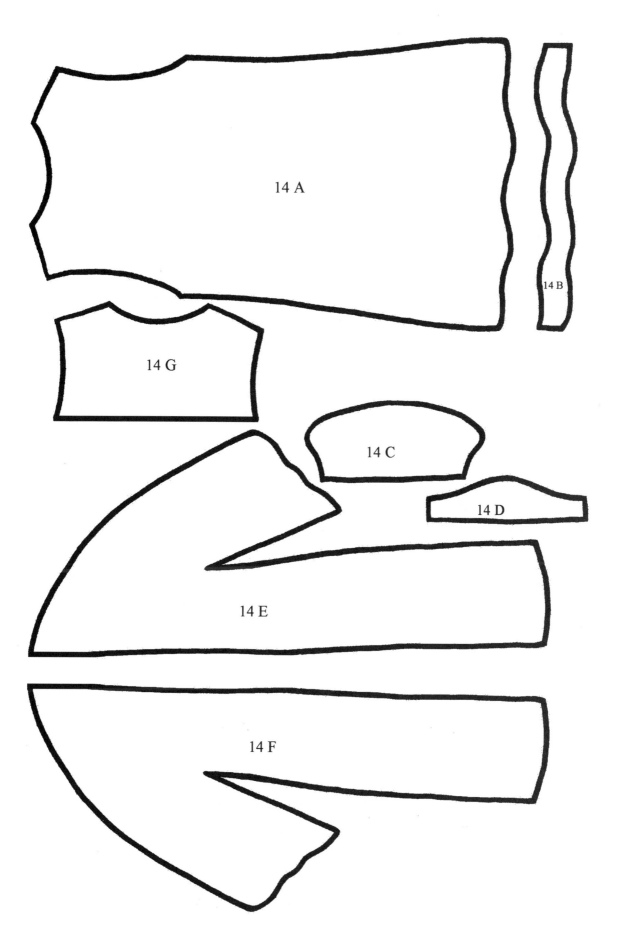

14 A

14 B

14 G

14 C

14 D

14 E

14 F

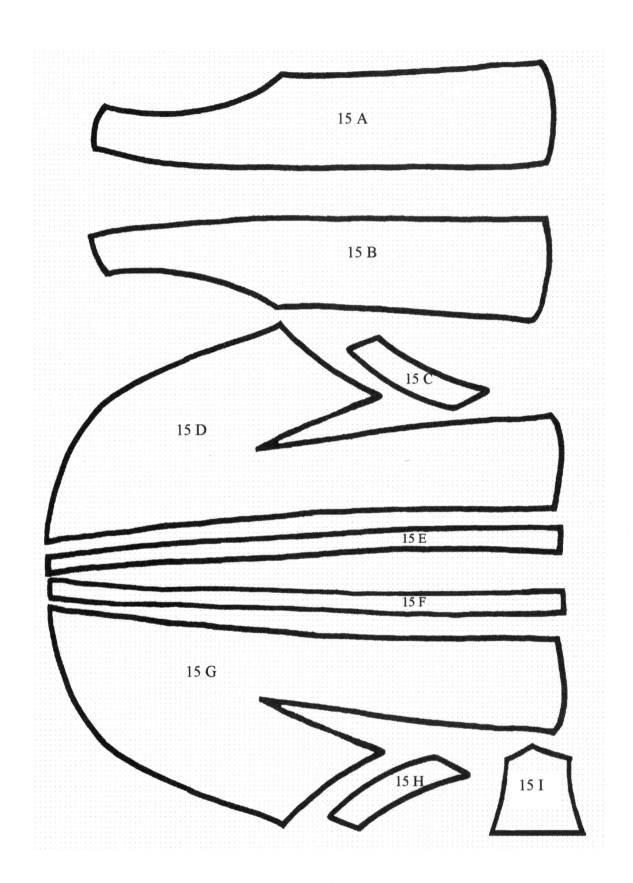

15 A

15 B

15 C

15 D

15 E

15 F

15 G

15 H

15 I

Photocopy or trace puppet patterns. Do not cut patterns from book.

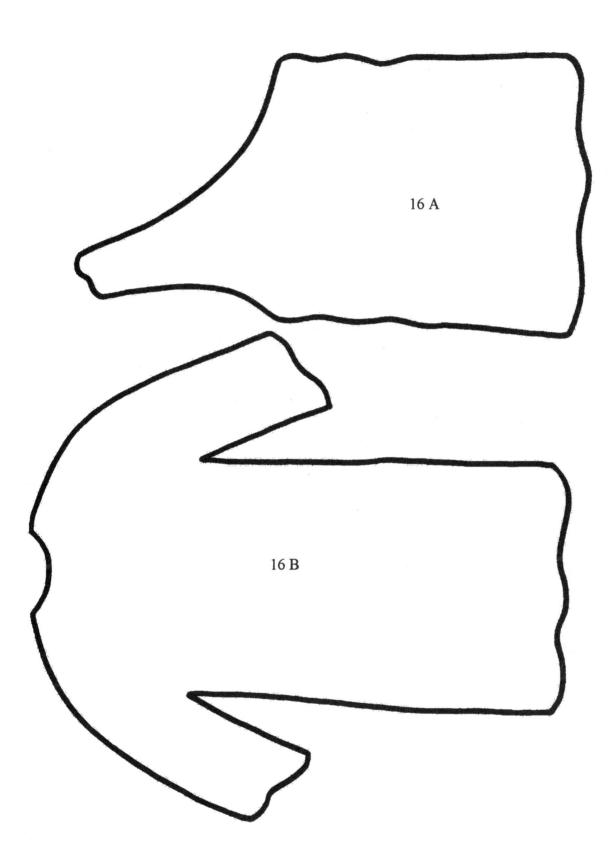

16 A

16 B

Photocopy or trace puppet patterns. Do not cut patterns from book.

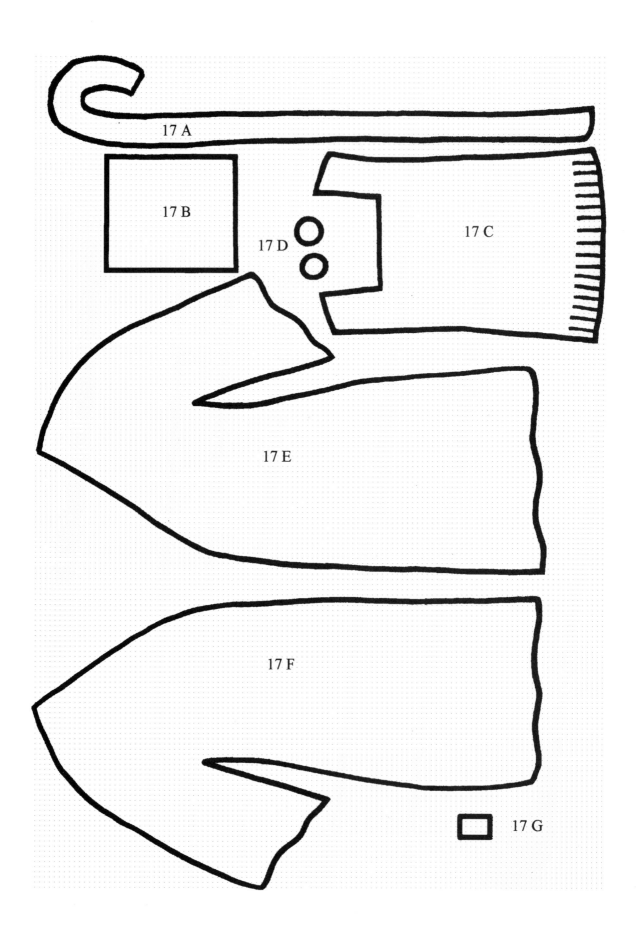

17 A

17 B

17 C

17 D

17 E

17 F

17 G

Photocopy or trace puppet patterns. Do not cut patterns from book.

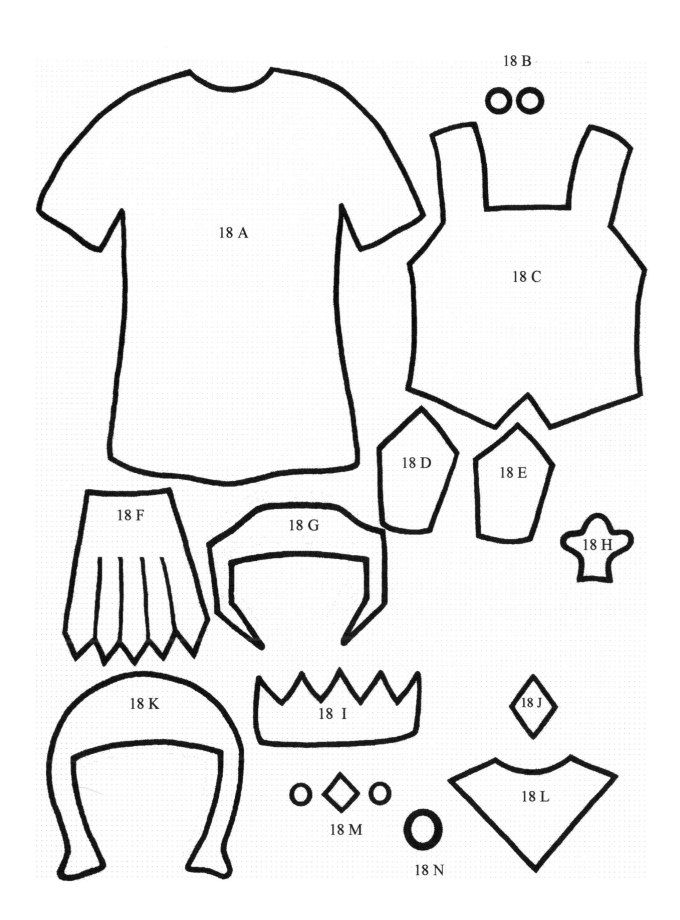

18 B

18 A

18 C

18 D   18 E

18 F   18 G   18 H

18 K   18 I   18 J

18 M   18 L

18 N

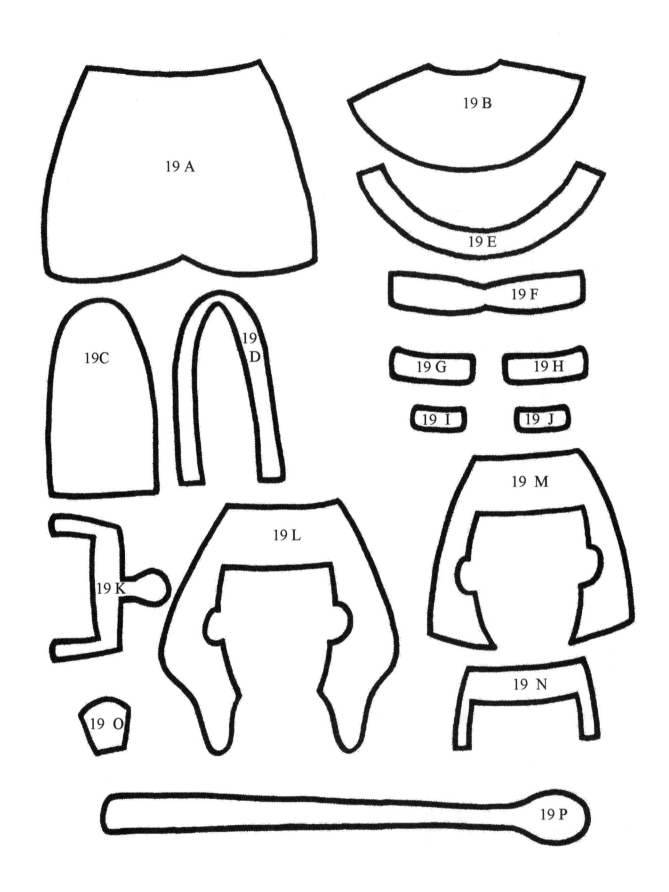

Photocopy or trace puppet patterns. Do not cut patterns from book.

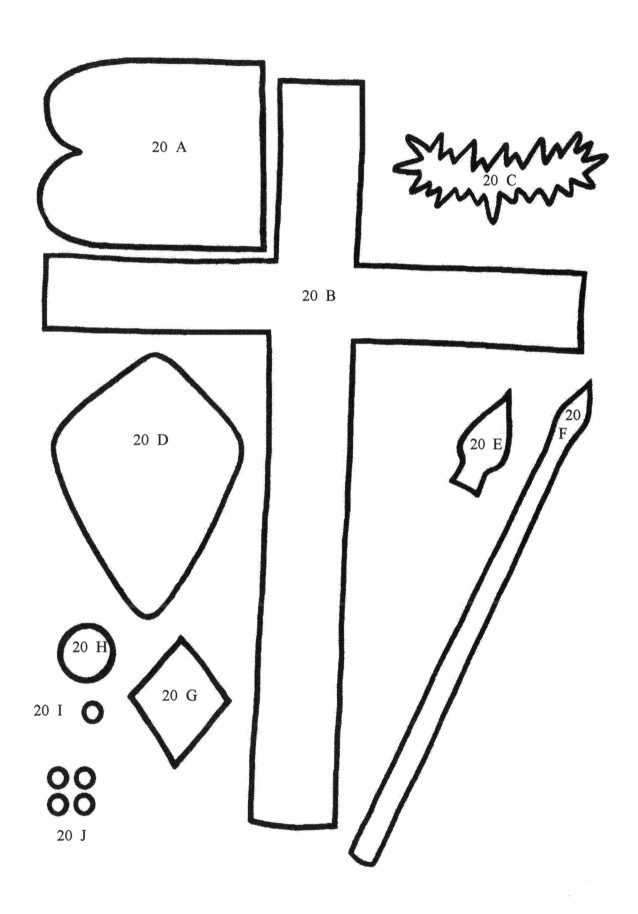

20 A

20 C

20 B

20 D

20 E

20 F

20 H

20 G

20 I

20 J

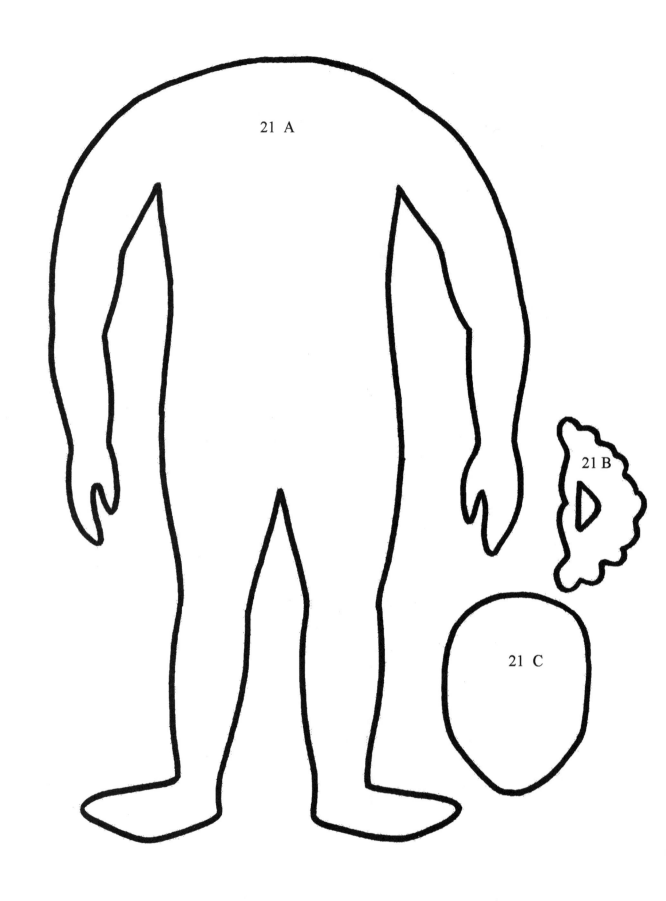

21 A

21 B

21 C

Photocopy or trace puppet patterns. Do not cut patterns from book.

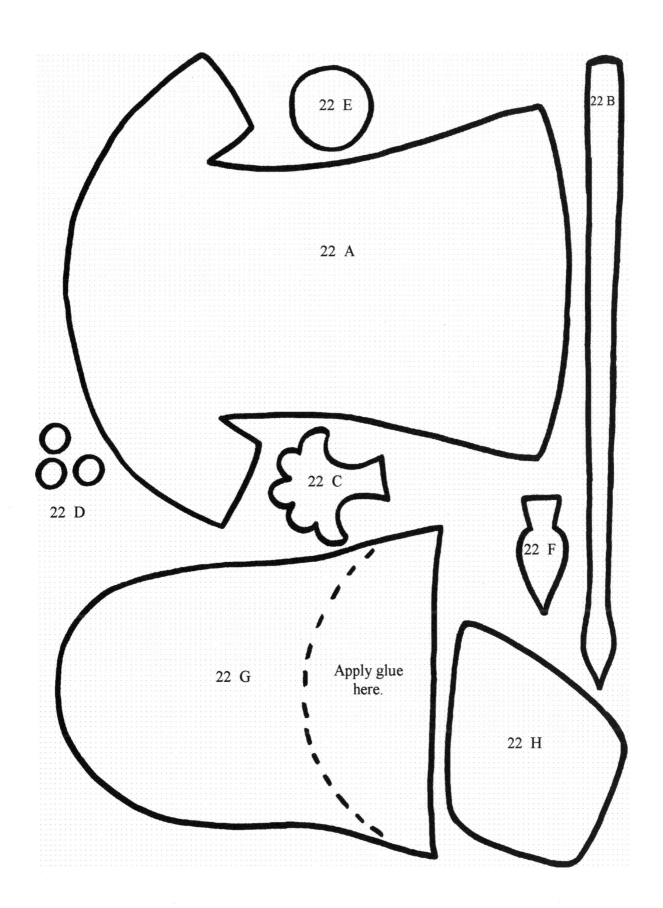

22 E

22 B

22 A

22 D

22 C

22 F

22 G

Apply glue here.

22 H

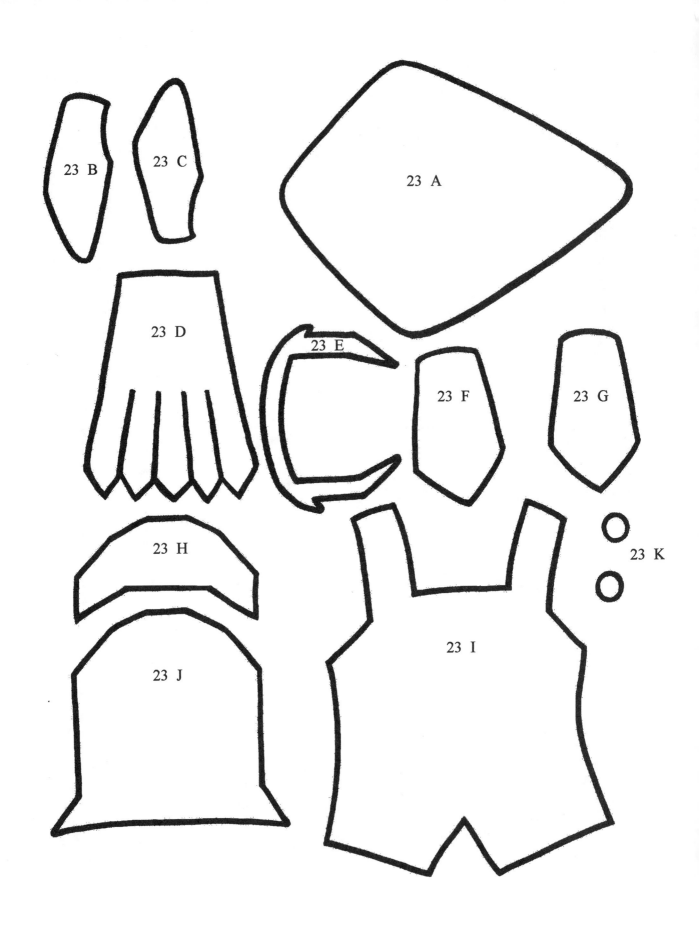

23 B

23 C

23 A

23 D

23 E

23 F

23 G

23 H

23 K

23 J

23 I

Photocopy or trace puppet patterns. Do not cut patterns from book.

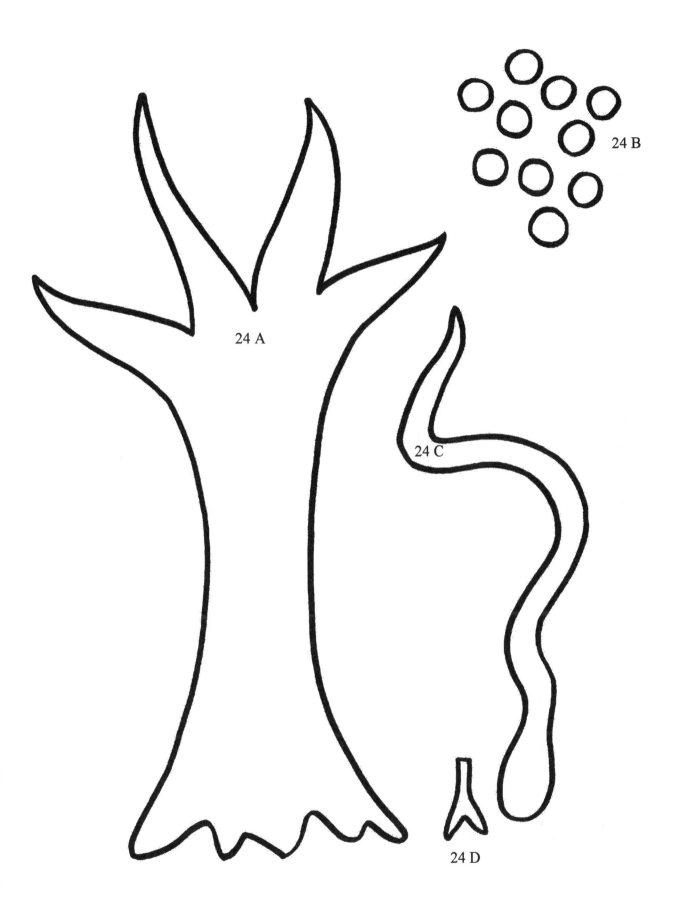

24 A

24 B

24 C

24 D

Photocopy or trace puppet patterns. Do not cut patterns from book.

25 A

25 B

Photocopy or trace puppet patterns. Do not cut patterns from book.

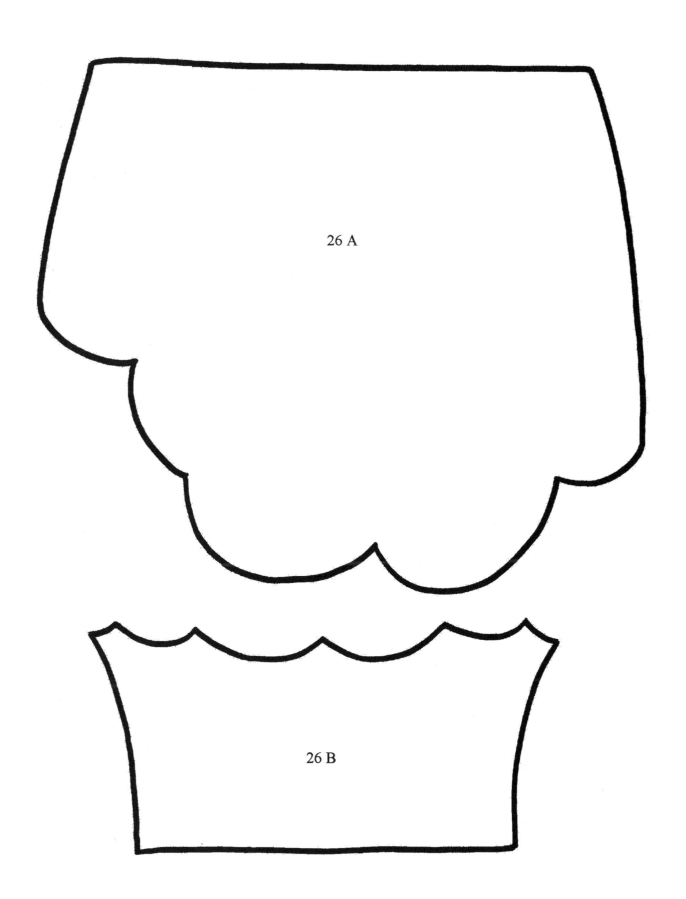

26 A

26 B

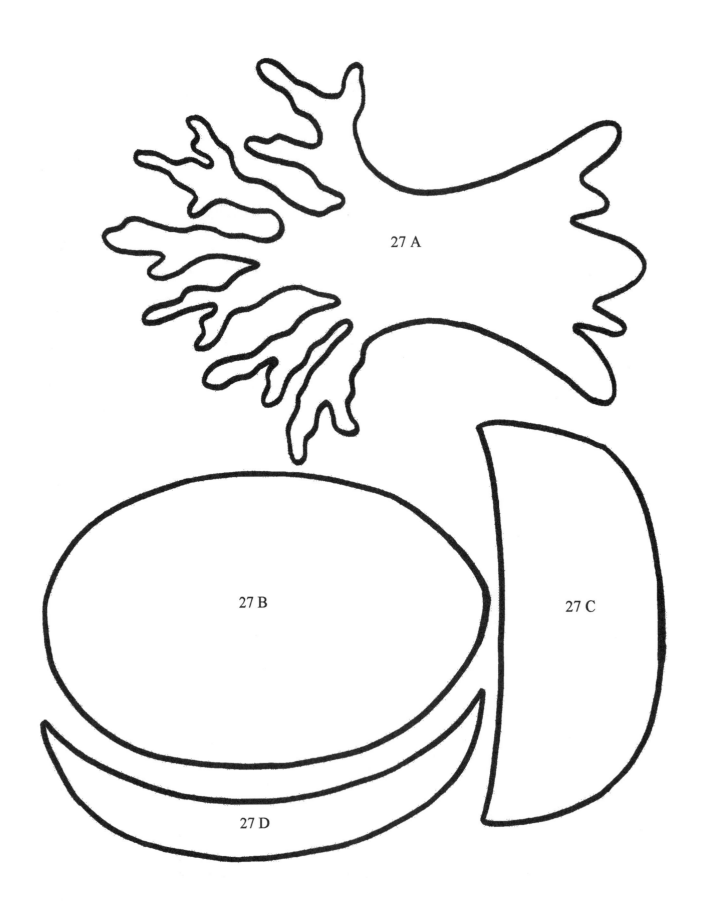

27 A

27 B

27 C

27 D

Photocopy or trace puppet patterns. Do not cut patterns from book.

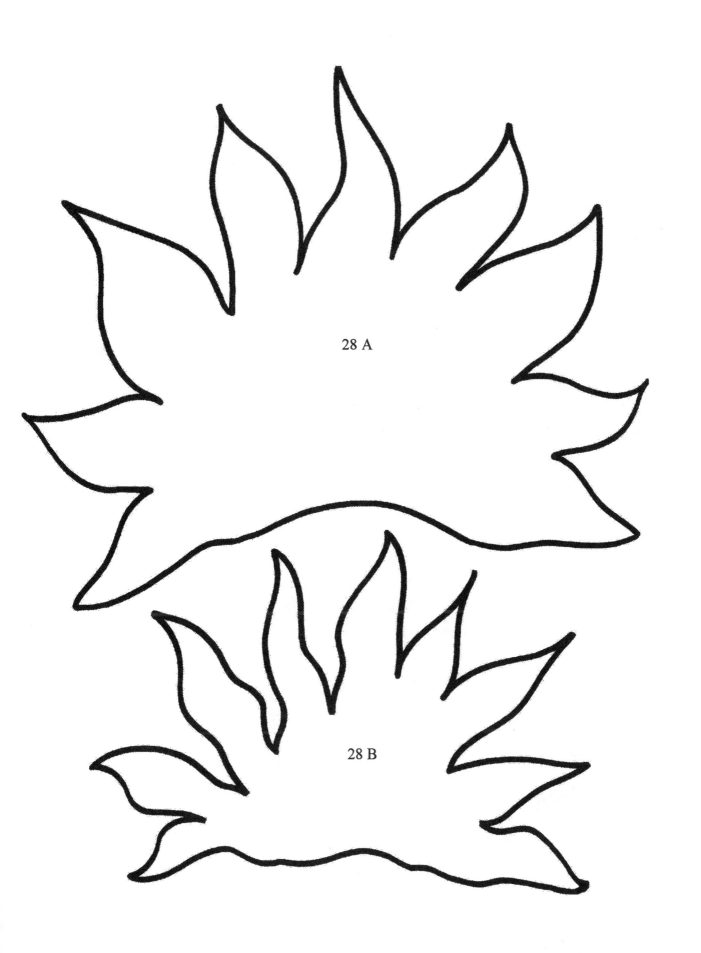

28 A

28 B

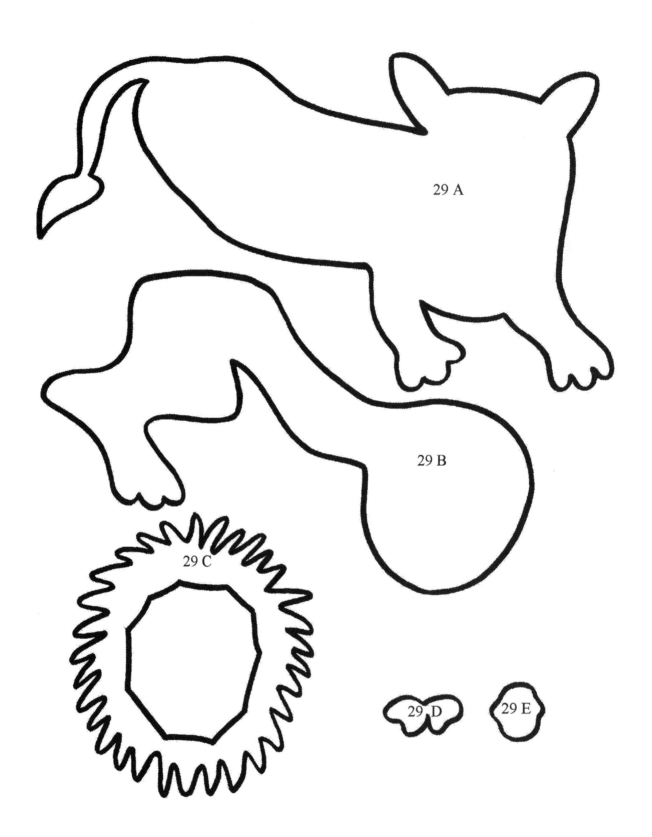

29 A

29 B

29 C

29 D   29 E

Photocopy or trace puppet patterns. Do not cut patterns from book.

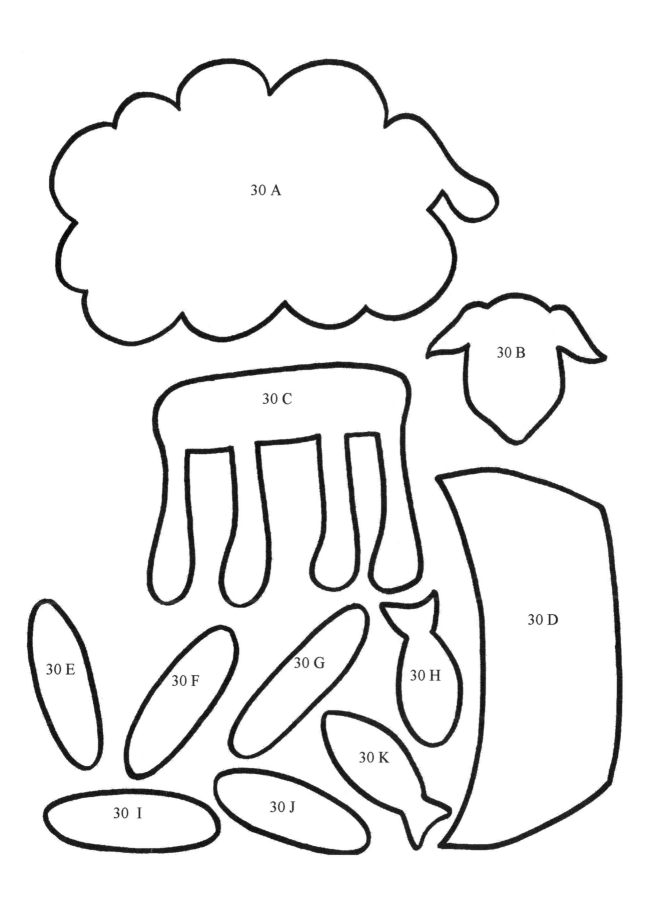

30 A

30 B

30 C

30 D

30 E

30 F

30 G

30 H

30 I

30 J

30 K

Photocopy or trace puppet patterns. Do not cut patterns from book.

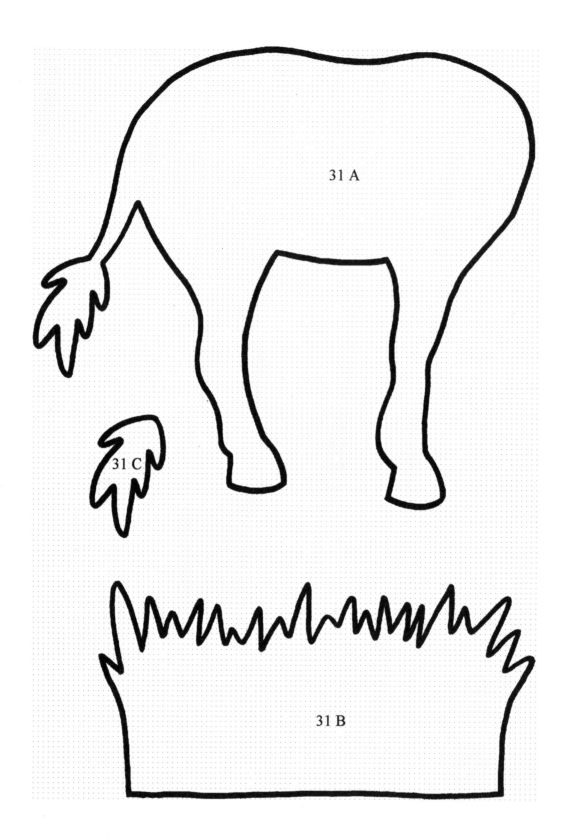

31 A

31 C

31 B

Photocopy or trace puppet patterns. Do not cut patterns from book.

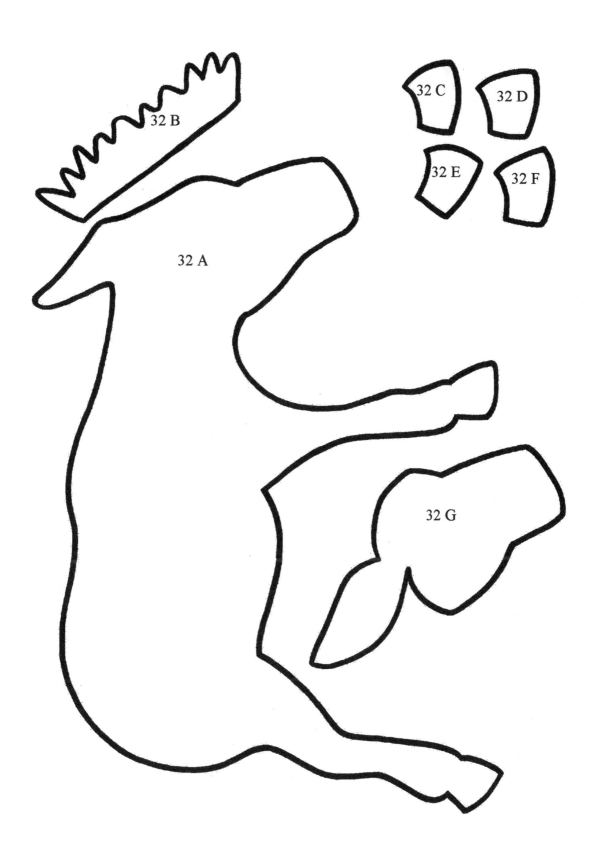

32 B

32 C

32 D

32 E

32 F

32 A

32 G

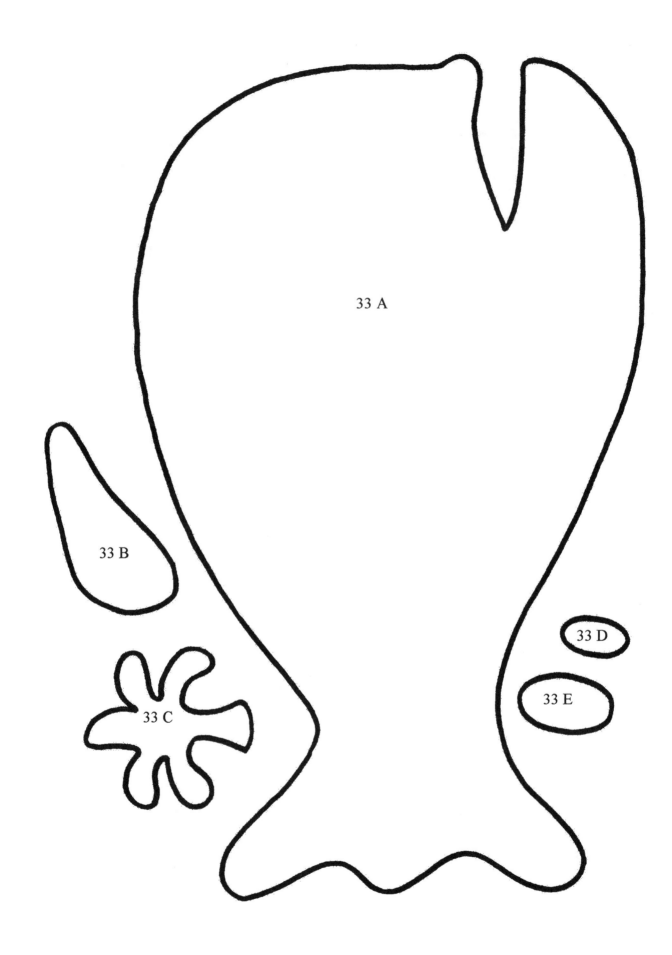

33 A

33 B

33 C

33 D

33 E

Photocopy or trace puppet patterns. Do not cut patterns from book.

34 H   34 I

34 A   34 C

34 B   34 D

34 F   34 G

34 E

Photocopy or trace puppet patterns. Do not cut patterns from book.   169

35 A

35 B

35 C

35 D

35 E

35 G

35 H

35 F

Photocopy or trace puppet patterns. Do not cut patterns from book.

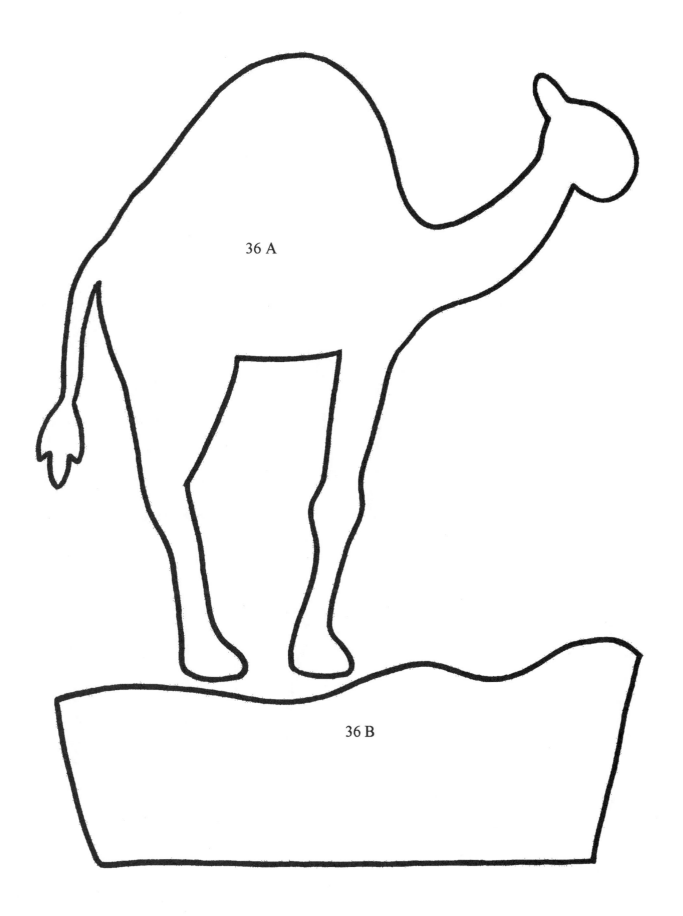

36 A

36 B

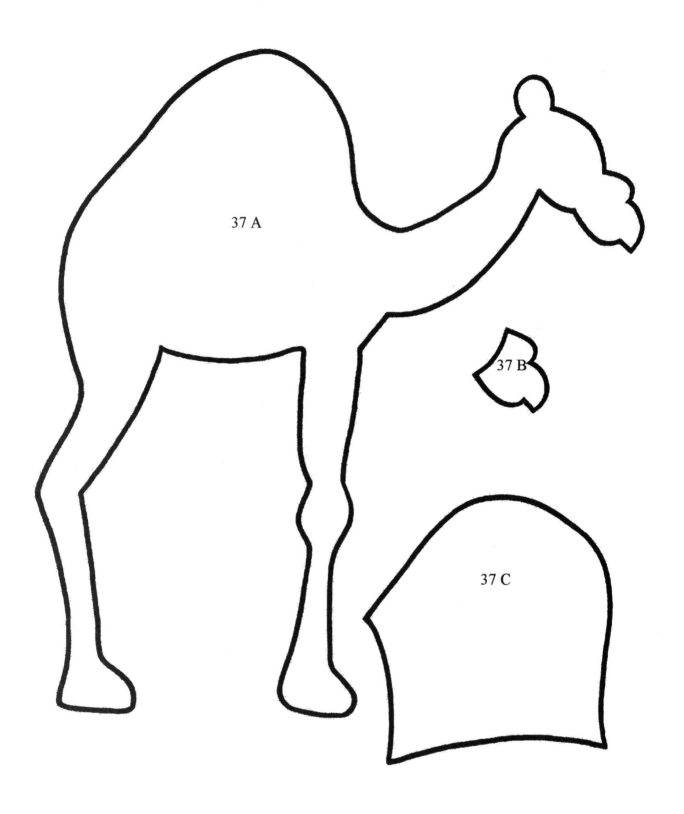

37 A

37 B

37 C

Photocopy or trace puppet patterns. Do not cut patterns from book.

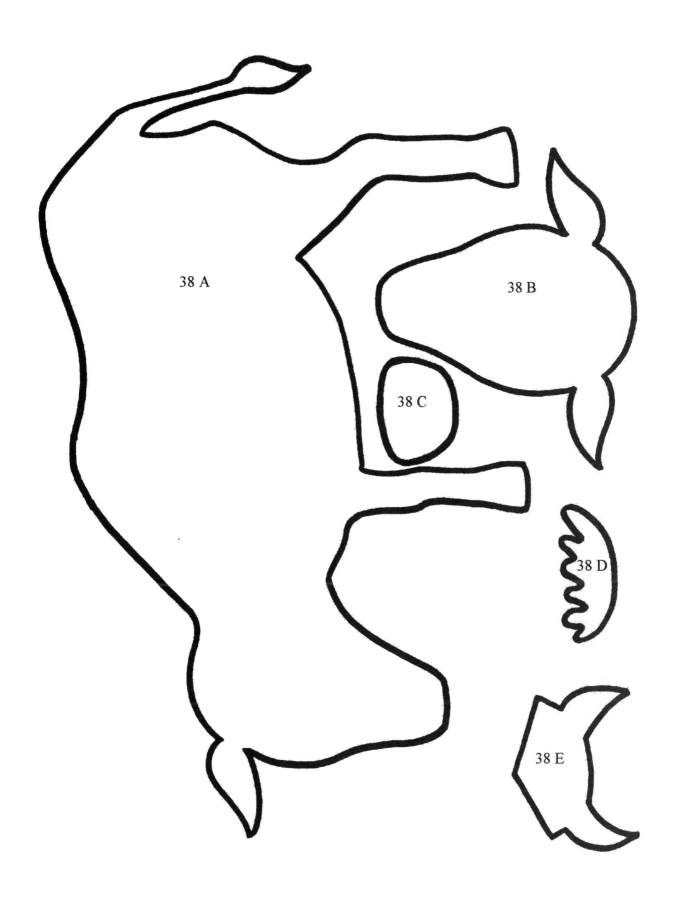

38 A

38 B

38 C

38 D

38 E

39 A

39 B 39 C 39 D 39 E

39 F

Photocopy or trace puppet patterns. Do not cut patterns from book.

Making the Most
of the Preschool Years

Educational psychologists claim that more than half of a child's learning occurs in his first few years. Valerie discusses how you can make the most of these important years. She also offers tips on multi-level teaching, including teaching school-aged children with a toddler in the house, as she draws from her own experience in teaching her six children.

Valerie offers 100 activities for preschoolers to encourage independent play. Complete with illustrations, patterns, and diagrams! $20.00

Visit us at www.ValerieBendt.com

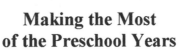

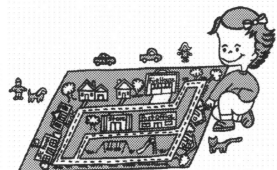

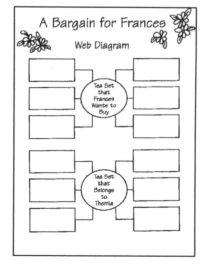

Creating Books with Children

In this six week, book-making unit study your children will study authors and illustrators while creating their own books. These books will become lifetime treasures! You will use this book again and again. Many subject areas are covered.

Week 1: Prewriting activities
Week 2: Writing the stories
Week 3: Text layout and editing
Week 4: Illustrating the books
Week 5: Developing the beginning and ending pages and the book jackets.
Week 6: Assembling the books   **$20.00**

Visit us at www.ValerieBendt.com

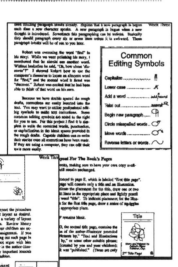

Creating Books with Children
2-Disc DVD Set

This professionally produced, 2-disc set includes Valerie's popular workshop "Making Memorable Books with Children" as well as step-by-step instructions for making a mock-up book, laying out the book pages, creating decorative book jackets, developing the skeleton pages, making hardbound cloth book covers, and binding the books.

Valerie offers plenty of how-to-tips to ensure bookmaking success, as well as more than 50 sample pages from books made by her children.

This 2-disc DVD set is an audio-visual companion to Valerie's best selling book *Creating Books with Children*.

DVD Set $24.00

Visit us at www.ValerieBendt.com

Successful Puppet Making

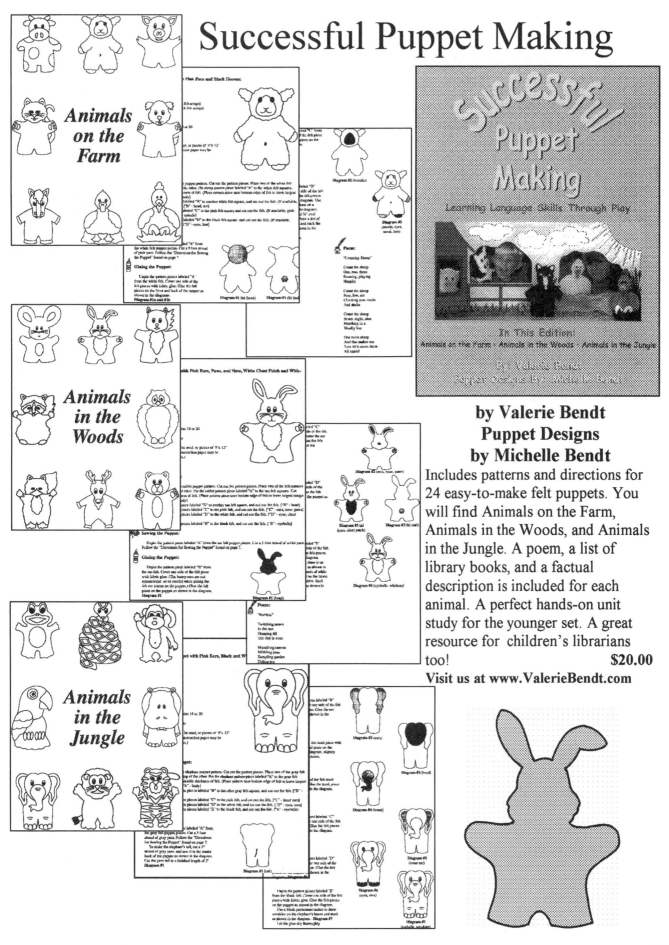

by Valerie Bendt
Puppet Designs
by Michelle Bendt

Includes patterns and directions for 24 easy-to-make felt puppets. You will find Animals on the Farm, Animals in the Woods, and Animals in the Jungle. A poem, a list of library books, and a factual description is included for each animal. A perfect hands-on unit study for the younger set. A great resource for children's librarians too! **$20.00**

Visit us at www.ValerieBendt.com

Reading Made Easy
A Guide to Teach Your Child to Read
by Valerie Bendt, author of *How to Create Your Own Unit Study*

- ◆ Phonics based
- ◆ 108 easy lessons
- ◆ 3 lessons per week
- ◆ Less than 30 minutes a day
- ◆ Fully scripted
- ◆ Christian content
- ◆ Original stories and poems

- ◆ Introduction to punctuation and capitalization
- ◆ Hands-on activities
- ◆ Writing and drawing activities
- ◆ Homeschool family tested
- ◆ 512 pages

Lesson 22

Materials: reading manual, index cards, pen, gray crayon, and black crayon.

Instructions: In today's lesson the child will review the following words from previous lessons: *nap, hat, rag, ham, dad, pan, sack, back, sail, pain, game, gave, rake, late, hay, say, day, may, way,* and *pay.* He will also review the following sight words: *is, was, to, has* and *the.*

The child will read the following sentences and complete a variety of exercises based on the sentences: *The rat is sad. The rat has a rake. The rat can rake the hay.*

Dialogue: Read the words below. Remember that the dotted letters are silent. They make no sound.

nap   hat   rag

ham   dad   pan

sack   back   sail

pain   game   gave

rake   late   hay

say   day   may

        way   pay

Read the sight words below.

is   was   to

has   the

Read the sentences below, and then I will show you a picture that goes with the sentences. (Run your finger under each word as the child reads.)

The rat is sad.

The rat has a rake.

The rat can rake the hay.

Now I will show you the picture of the rat.

What is the rat holding? That's right, he is holding a rake. What is the rat doing with the rake? Yes, he is raking the hay. Why do you think that the rat is sad? Yes, he is probably sad, because he has a lot of hay to rake.

- ◆ Portions of the text to be read aloud by the parent are printed in this special font.

> Read

- ◆ Sight words are underlined in black.

> The

- ◆ Short vowels are printed in gray.

> a

- ◆ A simple picture accompanies the story, followed by comprehension questions.

- ◆ Actual page size is 8 ½" x 11".

Only $45.00

- ◆ Long vowels are printed in bold black. **a**

- ◆ Silent letters are printed in a dotted style.

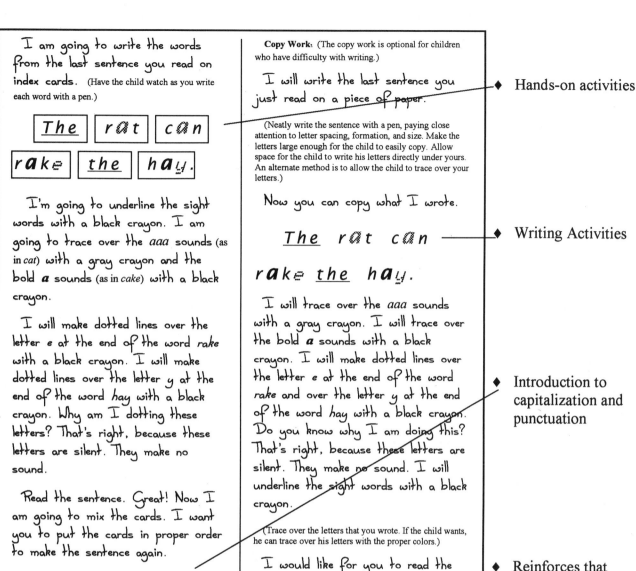

I am going to write the words from the last sentence you read on index cards. (Have the child watch as you write each word with a pen.)

| The | rat | can |

| rake | the | hay. |

I'm going to underline the sight words with a black crayon. I am going to trace over the *aaa* sounds (as in *cat*) with a gray crayon and the bold *a* sounds (as in *cake*) with a black crayon.

I will make dotted lines over the letter *e* at the end of the word *rake* with a black crayon. I will make dotted lines over the letter *y* at the end of the word *hay* with a black crayon. Why am I dotting these letters? That's right, because these letters are silent. They make no sound.

Read the sentence. Great! Now I am going to mix the cards. I want you to put the cards in proper order to make the sentence again.

(Assist the child with putting the cards in proper order. Remind him if necessary that a sentence begins with an uppercase letter and ends with a period.)

Now read the sentence.

Copy Work: (The copy work is optional for children who have difficulty with writing.)

I will write the last sentence you just read on a piece of paper.

(Neatly write the sentence with a pen, paying close attention to letter spacing, formation, and size. Make the letters large enough for the child to easily copy. Allow space for the child to write his letters directly under yours. An alternate method is to allow the child to trace over your letters.)

Now you can copy what I wrote.

The rat can

rake the hay.

I will trace over the *aaa* sounds with a gray crayon. I will trace over the bold *a* sounds with a black crayon. I will make dotted lines over the letter *e* at the end of the word *rake* and over the letter *y* at the end of the word *hay* with a black crayon. Do you know why I am doing this? That's right, because these letters are silent. They make no sound. I will underline the sight words with a black crayon.

(Trace over the letters that you wrote. If the child wants, he can trace over his letters with the proper colors.)

I would like for you to read the sentence once more. Very good! Would you like to draw a picture to go with your sentence? Now let's read a book together.

2

♦ Hands-on activities

♦ Writing Activities

♦ Introduction to capitalization and punctuation

♦ Reinforces that reading is important and enjoyable

*"**Reading Made Easy** is a wonderful book! The lessons are short and easy to retain, which results in a contagious sense of accomplishment. Not only does **Reading Made Easy** inspire and make learning fun; it is also easy and fun for this 'mom' teacher as well. A great book with terrific plans and activities."* Kathy Pelham, Tampa, Florida

*"**Reading Made Easy** concludes with Mrs. Bendt's, twelve-chapter short story, **Gideon's Gift.** This heartfelt story emphasizes the joy of reading and writing while stressing the significance of giving God the glory in all situations and finding our God given gifts. Each chapter's suspenseful conclusion urges the child on to the next lesson. This beautifully written account exposes the child to vocabulary not normally used in today's books for children."* Cathy Pierce – Children's Librarian

Visit us at www.ValerieBendt.com

Unit Studies Made Easy

A Guide to Simplified Learning at Home

Valerie Bendt's popular book, *How to Create Your Own Unit Study,* is back! This updated, expanded version includes all four of Valerie's previously published unit study books in one big volume:

- *How to Create Your Own Unit Study*
- *The Unit Study Idea Book*
- *For the Love of Reading*
- *Success with Unit Studies*
- Plus a new section entitled *Biblical Parenting or Schooling at Home?*
- **336 pages**
- **$30.00**

- Are you tired of trying to teach like the schools?
- Are you searching for a simple yet effective teaching method?
- Do you want to instill a love of learning in your children?
- This guide presents the nuts and bolts of teaching through unit studies.
- Learn how you and your children can create your own unit studies
- Includes more than 20 units to get you started right away!

Visit us at www.ValerieBendt.com

Easy-to-Make Bible Story Puppets includes patterns and directions for making 40 felt hand puppets. Children enjoy acting out scenes from their favorite Bible stories, thus aiding in memory retention, vocabulary development, and language skills. The puppets are inexpensive, easy to make, and durable, making them a truly valuable resource. $28.00

Baby Jesus (Yeshua)

Possible Characters: Baby Jesus. The baby can be used as any baby if you omit the bed of hay. The baby can be made without a puppet background and can be held by another puppet.

Materials:

- 2 light blue felt squares for puppet background
- 1 yellow felt square for bed of hay
- Peach colored felt scraps for baby's face
- Brown colored felt scraps for baby's hair
- 1 medium blue colored felt square for baby blanket and baby's body
- Light blue embroidery thread
- Scissors
- Straight pins or masking tape
- Large tapestry needle, size 18 or 20
- Fabric glue
- Puppet Background A on page 133. Pattern pieces 7 A, 7 B, 7 C, 7 D, and 7 E on page 142.

Directions

Sew the puppet background according to the directions on page 5. Photocopy or trace the Baby Jesus pieces, and cut them out. Pin or tape the pattern pieces to the felt, and then cut the felt. Rolled pieces of masking tape can be attached at several points to the back of each pattern piece. This will enable the pattern piece to stick to the felt while cutting. Follow the directions beside each diagram for cutting and gluing the pattern pieces. You may want to cut out all the felt pieces, and practice placing them on the puppet before gluing each piece in place.

Attach pattern piece 7A to the yellow felt, and cut the felt. Remove the pattern piece from the felt. Cut a ring of fringe around the felt piece as indicated in the diagram and as shown on the pattern piece. Cover one side of the felt with fabric glue, leaving the fringed parts free from glue. Glue the felt piece on the puppet as shown in the diagram.

 pieces 7 B and 7 E to the ... felt, and cut out the felt. Remove ... B from the medium blue felt ... of the felt with fabric glue, and ... ece on the puppet as shown in the ... pattern piece 7 E for the next

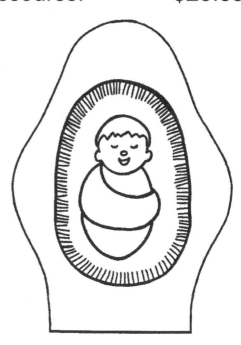

... Cover one ... medium blue felt. Cover one side of the felt with fabric glue, and glue the felt piece on the puppet as shown in the diagram.

Attach pattern piece 7 C to the peach felt, and cut out the felt. Remove the pattern piece from the felt. Cover one side of the felt with fabric glue, and glue the felt piece on the puppet as shown in the diagram.

Attach pattern piece 7 D to the brown felt, and cut out the felt. Remove the pattern piece from the felt. Cover one side of the felt with fabric glue, and glue the felt piece on the puppet as shown in the diagram.

Add facial features using three-dimensional fabric paint, permanent markers, or felt scraps.

Visit us at
www.ValerieBendt.com

183

Valerie Bendt's Workshop Topics

Making the Most of the Preschool Years (Y)
Educational psychologists claim that more than half of a child's learning occurs in his first few years. Should we take advantage of our preschooler's ability to absorb information by engaging him in academics, or would another course of action be more productive? Valerie discusses how you can make the most of these important years. Valerie also offers tips on multi-level teaching, including teaching school-aged children with a toddler in the house, as she draws from her own experience in teaching her six children.
45 – 60 minutes

Reading Made Easy (Y)
Valerie offers key information to help demystify reading instruction. She covers simple steps that can be immediately put into practice to help you effectively teach your child to read. Valerie takes instruction one step further as she offers ideas to help your child not only learn to read — but learn to love to read. For it's when our children learn to love to read that they become lifelong learners!
The ideas presented in this workshop are based on Valerie's phonics instruction book, *Reading Made Easy*, but can be used to enhance any reading program.
45 – 60 minutes

Introduction to Unit Studies (G)
As she reviews the basics of teaching by the unit study method, Valerie gives instruction on how to develop unit studies based on your own family's needs and desires. Valerie offers anecdotes and samples from unit studies she has done with her family. Rekindle a love for learning in your family. Encourage creativity, expression, and individuality. Put away tedious textbooks and get on with real learning and real life!
45 – 60 minutes

Making Memorable Books with Children (G)
Valerie presents an upbeat introduction to creating books with your children that will be treasured for a lifetime. This workshop is based on Valerie's popular book, *Creating Books with Children*, which is a six-week, book-making unit study. Valerie offers numerous tips and techniques to encourage your children to write and illustrate effectively. These are tips that you can put into practice right away. No more, "I can't write and I can't draw!" (This workshop is also of interest to children)
45 – 60 minutes

Homeschooling or Schooling at Home (G)
When Valerie began homeschooling more than 20 years ago, she realized she couldn't effectively re-create school in the home. More importantly she learned that she shouldn't. Valerie explains that homeschooling is more than an educational alternative, it is a lifestyle. Join her as she offers practical ways to energize your homeschool and encourage your family to be life-long learners. She will also share the educational experiences of her six children, including the post high school endeavors of her four oldest children. Valerie wants to show you that you can go the distance!
45 – 60 minutes

About the Speaker: Valerie Bendt
Valerie and her husband, Bruce, have homeschooled their six children all of their school lives. Valerie has written the following books of interest to homeschoolers: *Unit Studies Made Easy, Creating Books with Children, The Frances Study Guide, Successful Puppet Making, Reading Made Easy, Making the Most of the Preschool Years,* and *Easy-to-Make Bible Story Puppets.* Valerie and Bruce's four oldest children have graduated from homeschooling, and the Bendts continue to homeschool their other children. The family resides in Tampa, Florida.
To inquire about speaking engagements please contact Valerie at: Phone: 813-758-6793
Regular Mail: 333 W. Rio Vista Court, Tampa, FL 33604-6940 or Email: ValerieBendt@earthlink.net.
(Y) – Suitable for those with younger children – including preschoolers and children learning to read.
(G) – Suitable for those with children of all ages – particularly elementary aged and up.
www.ValerieBendt.com